Books by David Ogilvy

BLOOD, BRAINS & BEER

BLOOD, BRAINS & BEER

The Autobiography of

DAVID OGILVY

NEW YORK *Atheneum* 1978

"Toad's Song" is from *The Wind in the Willows* by Kenneth Grahame, copyright 1908 Charles Scribner's Sons. Reprinted with permission of Charles Scribner's Sons.

The passage in chapter 3 from Ruth Gordon's *Myself Among Others*, published by Atheneum, © 1970, 1971 by T.F.T. Corporation, is reprinted by permission.

Library of Congress Cataloging in Publication Data

Ogilvy, David, 1911–
Blood, brains and beer.

   Includes index.
   1. Ogilvy, David, 1911–   2. Advertising—
Biography. I. Title.
HF58.O34A32   1977   659.1'092'4 [B]   77-76541
ISBN 0-689-10809-5

Toad's Song

The world has held great Heroes,
  As history books have showed;
But never a name to go down to fame
  Compared with that of Toad!

The clever men at Oxford
  Know all that there is to be knowed.
But they none of them know one half as much
  As intelligent Mr. Toad!

The animals sat in the Ark and cried,
  Their tears in torrents flowed.
Who was it said, "There's land ahead"?
  Encouraging Mr. Toad!

The Army all saluted
  As they marched along the road.
Was it the King? Or Kitchener?
  No. It was Mr. Toad.

The Queen and her Ladies-in-waiting
  Sat at the window and sewed.
She cried, "Look! who's that handsome man?"
  They answered, "Mr. Toad."

The Wind in the Willows by Kenneth Grahame

Contents

BLOOD, BRAINS & BEER

⌈1⌋

Sweet Master

M Y grandfather was born on June 23. So was my father. And so was I. In 1911.

Our home was in Horsley, a village in Surrey about thirty miles southwest of London. In those days Surrey was still a paradise of plovers' eggs, cowslip wine, charcoal burners, gypsies in caravans, thatched haystacks, and governess carts. There was also a witch called Dame Feathers who lived in a chalk-pit. Our next-door neighbor was Sir Henry Roscoe the chemist, and his niece Beatrix Potter was a frequent visitor to our house. Her England is the England I remember.

In the eyes of Nancy Niggins, my nanny, I could

3

do no wrong. When my elder brother and sisters complained that I was intolerable, she defended me—"Sweet Master, he's *hungry*." When I swallowed the castor oil instead of spewing it on her bed, she saluted me—"Sweet Master is braver than Lord Roberts."*

The undernurse was heard to snarl, "Wait until I get hold of you!" This turned out to be no idle threat. When I was three, England declared war on Germany, my father was ruined, and his servants were sacked—Brett the gardener, Bashford the chauffeur, Florence Cherry the housemaid, Lucy Skull the cook who specialized in meringues, and, worst of all, Nancy Niggins. She was my surrogate mother, and her departure was a trauma from which I have not recovered. The only survivor of this holocaust was the aforesaid undernurse. She lost no time in making my life miserable. Her strategy was to attack my self-confidence by convincing me that I was a runt, a weakling, a milksop, and a mollycoddle. When my sister Mary wrestled me to the ground, this termagant held me up to derision, making no allowance for the fact that Mary was four years older than me.

We had to move in with my mother's mother in London. This plunged my father into a permanent sulk. Grandmother said *serviette* when she

* Commander in chief of the British Army in the Boer War.

should have said table napkin, mirror when she should have said looking glass. She pronounced venison, medicine and vegetable in three syllables. Rebecca West, who was her niece, has described her as looking like a cross between a bloodhound and a woman policeman.* But I loved her gusto. She had long since banished my errant grandfather, and I saw him only on expeditions to Madame Tussaud's waxworks:

Every night when the clock strikes one
They all come together with a rum-tum-tum,
Murderers, clergymen, thieves, and Lords,
Ever so jolly in Madame Tussaud's.

This grandfather, Arthur Fairfield, was an Irishman from County Kerry. He had been a civil servant, but was forced to resign when Joe Chamberlain caught him conniving with our cousins in Kerry for improvements to the Dingle harbor. His brother Edward Fairfield, an undersecretary at the Colonial Office, was accused of authorizing the Jameson Raid which triggered the Boer War, but died of a heart attack the night before he was to be questioned by the commission of inquiry. The *Times* wrote a generous obituary, exonerating him of blame, but my cantankerous grandfather would have none of it. He telegraphed to the editor: HOW DARE YOU IMPLY THAT ANYONE COULD

* In *The Fountain Overflows.*

5

FOR ONE MOMENT HAVE THOUGHT THAT MY BROTHER WAS IN ANY WAY CONNECTED WITH THAT PIRATICAL ENTERPRISE?

Driving to a dinner party in a hansom cab, he accused the driver of going a long way round, shouting such insults through the aperture in the roof that the man pulled up and forced Grandfather to get out and fight. When I was no more than five, he lectured me on the villainies of Mr. Gladstone, a kinsman of my father's, alleging that the Gladstone fortune derived from the slave trade. He was also fond of haranguing me on the Armenian atrocities.

Life with Grandmother was spoiled not only by my nurse, but also by the Zeppelin raids. They happened at night, but I also remember the first daylight raid on July 17, 1917—I could see the bombers, like a swarm of bees high above.

One day when I was six, my mother's sister Zoë Fairfield took me to a garden party at the headquarters of the Student Christian Movement, which she managed.* An African bishop spent the afternoon playing bowls with me. No grownup had ever been so nice before; obviously black people were a superior race. During our communal

---

* If my aunt had been a man, she would have become an archbishop. Dr. James Parkes, the religious historian, writes that "the contribution she made to the developing ecumenism of British Christianity was immeasurable" (*Voyage of Discoveries*, Gollancz).

bath that evening, I instructed my sisters to pinch me, and to keep pinching until I was black. They were able to turn my right leg a beautiful brown, and a few days later they had finished the left leg, but by that time the right one had returned to pink.

I was the original Nosey Parker. At the age of eight I formed the habit of asking my father's friends how much they were worth; most of them were so taken aback that they told me. And I devoted one day during every school vacation to reading my eldest sister's love letters. This genius for espionage was to come in useful during the Hitler war.

I always preferred the company of grownups, the older the more interesting. My particular friend was Canon Wilson, who had been a friend of Charles Stuart Calverly at Cambridge in 1852. He knew all Calverly's poems by heart, and laboriously taught them to me:

The auld wife sat at her ivied door
(Butter and eggs and a pound of cheese)
A thing she had frequently done before;
And her spectacles lay on her apron'd knees.

My father was kind, patient, gentle, straightforward, unselfish, affectionate, athletic, and strong as an ox. He sneezed louder than anyone I have ever known, ate spoonfuls of hot Colman's mustard without any apparent sign of distress, and climbed trees as fast as a chimpanzee. He did his best to make me as strong and brainy as himself. When I was six, he required that I should drink a glass of raw blood every day. To strengthen my mental faculties, he ordained that I should eat calves' brains three times a week, washed down with a bottle of beer. Blood, brains and beer; a noble experiment.

He admired all his children without reservation. When a schoolmaster dared to write something critical on my report card, my father said, "The man is an ass." Soon after I started my first job in advertising, I wrote to tell him that my salary had been doubled; next time I went to visit him, he was waiting at the door of his cottage, chanting "See the Conquering Hero Comes." But he was not blind to my shortcomings. When I was fourteen I made the mistake of sending him an overblown poem I had composed:

The glory of the sunset is roaring in the West
Day is going, night coming, and they meet breast
*   to breast*
And linger in one blazing kiss of fire and cloud
Both mistress of the world, both radiant and proud.

How, he wanted to know, could Day, which disappeared in the West, come face to face with Night, which came from the East? When I was twenty-three I sent him a copy of a fifty-page report I had written on the marketing operations of Allied Ironfounders. His only reaction was to point out the spelling mistakes. When I asked him to take me on one of his fishing expeditions in the Jura, he refused—"You are too impatient to fish, you would drive me mad." When a rich cousin invited me to shoot pheasants on his estate, I asked my father to lend me a pair of his guns. "No," he replied, "shooting is a rich man's sport and you are not a rich man." When I was at Oxford, he urged me to stop buying an evening paper on the grounds that I could not afford the penny it cost.

From my father I inherited two things—smoking a pipe and a scatological sense of humor. I was devoted to him, but we never had a conversation of any intimacy, even after I grew up. He was a classical scholar, and had taught himself to speak Gaelic as well as English. He sang Gaelic songs with overwhelming pathos, and played the bagpipes—not reels and marches, but pibroch, those intricate variations which are the highest form of bagpipe music. He had played rugby football for Cambridge University. He was a crack shot with a rifle and spent his bachelor vacations stalking chamoix in the Pyrenees and stags in Scotland; our house was festooned with trophies. But by the time I knew him his self-confidence had been eroded by years of financial anxiety. He saw himself as a failure, and it gnawed at his vitals. He had been wrapped up in his mother; their favorite game was to see whether he could dance reels faster than she could play them on the piano. He did not marry until he was thirty-five and then chose the wrong wife. My mother was a medical student of nineteen, with brown eyes, freckles, an eighteen-inch waist, a splendid bust, and a convoluted mind. She was to bear him five children, but I never saw any sign that she loved him. My father bored her to distraction. He took her nagging with too much patience and continued to treat her with dogged devotion for forty-two years. When she died, he died a fortnight later. I had promised to scatter his ashes in the deer forest where he had been happiest, but when the time came I funked that grisly rite.

My mother always resented the fact that her marriage to my father had prevented her becoming a doctor, and never found any other interest to occupy her restless mind. She was blind to all forms of art. She read continuously, starting every book on the last page and working her way back to the beginning. She detested dishes which contained onion or any other flavor. She had no talent for pleasure, but was never dull. Her favorite bedtime story was a serial about a family which suffered the embarrassment of having a grandmother who was a pig, by name Betsy Bumpher. The plot revolved around the problems which arose when Grandma Bumpher came to visit. Where, for example, should she sleep? If she were put in the pigsty, her feelings might be hurt, but if she were given a bedroom . . . It did not dawn on me until recently that Betsy Bumpher was her mother.

It was typical of my mother that, when I was thirteen, she gave me the following advice: "Never allow a surgeon to operate on your piles. It hurts like billy-o, and the piles always come back." After I grew up she told me, "You have inherited my love of gardening, but your taste is utterly vulgar. You have no interest in the plants themselves, all you want is to make a *show*." One day when we were on a long walk, she said, "I have very little money, but I am leaving every penny to your sisters. This will help them leave their husbands if they are minded to do so." She gave me a bum steer only once. When I was sixteen we were standing in a dense crowd outside the Duomo in Florence, waiting for the flight of the mechanical pigeon which signals the arrival of the Holy Ghost. Suddenly I spied a girl, the most beautiful I had ever seen, and started elbowing my way through the crowd in her direction. "Don't be a juggins," said my mother, "you will see dozens as pretty as her before you leave Italy." I made the mistake of believing her. She used her nose the way other people use their eyes. When she wanted to know if her children were clean, she *sniffed* us. When dishes were handed to her at dinner, she picked them up and smelled them. (I have inherited her nose, and I have a good palate. During a recent tour of the Arthur D. Little tasting lab in Boston, I was handed two glasses of brandy and challenged to identify them. This gave me no difficulty: one was Martell and the other Christian Brothers. At a dinner party on his plantation in Maryland, Arthur Houghton bet me that I could not identify the wine. I tasted it and wondered why Arthur, the archconnoisseur, had such awful stuff in his cellar. It could only be because it had been produced in the neighborhood. "Maryland?" Right again. Arthur planted an orchard of peach trees, only to see them devoured by deer. Every fifty yards around the perimeter of the orchard he hung tin cans and filled them with tiger manure from the Washington zoo. The smell terrified the deer and the peach trees were saved. When he tried *lion* manure, the deer ignored it. They hadn't smelled tigers or lions for tens of thousands of years, but they knew that they could outrun lions.)

My father sent me to a London kindergarten dressed in a kilt. This struck the English boys as effeminate, and one of them tormented me until I punched him in the nose. When the teacher denounced me to my parents, my mother said that it was cowardly to resort to physical violence; next time somebody goaded me, I would do better to punish him with my *tongue*. I took this advice to heart, and was soon able to report that I could "get any boy in the school on the *rack* with my tongue." It took me forty years to cure this habit.

The Kaiser's war started when I was three. Embroidered postcards from Bashford, now in Flanders. Dreaming about the return of ice cream, if the sugar shortage ever came to an end. Motoring with convalescent soldiers, and sitting on the stump of an Anzac hero whose leg had been amputated below the knee. Being dragged, screaming with terror, to my first cinema. Being stoned by the Belgian children who were refugees in the house next door. Pretending that my favorite doll was not a German soldier, which he was, but a railway porter. Being taken to see the first tank on exhibition in Trafalgar Square, and catechizing Colonel Swinton who had invented it.

And then, after four years and three months of Armageddon, mafficking in the streets on Armistice Day, followed by the Peace Day celebrations in the grounds of Horsley Towers, and everybody singing "K-K-K-Katie, Beautiful Katie."

A year later, I was sent to a boarding school. I was nine. St. Cyprian's was too expensive for my father to afford, but the headmaster and his wife were aware that he had won a First in the classical tripos at Cambridge, and were prepared to bet on my winning similar academic honors. This would redound to their credit and thus boost their enrollment; so they took me at half the usual fee— and never forgave me for it.

The first night at St. Cyprian's, I observed that the other boys knelt down before getting into bed. I assumed that they were using their chamber pots; I had never seen anyone pray, because there had been no religion in my family since my grandparents became agnostics in 1870, the year after Thomas Huxley invented the word. When the matron was told that I had not prayed, she took me off to her bedroom and tried to explain the mysteries of revealed religion. But my incredulity was too much for her, and she gave it up as a bad job. The following morning was a Sunday. I had never been in a church before, and did not know the drill. When the chaplain finished his sermon, I applauded. However, I soon became deeply religious. During Easter week I went about with a heavy heart, and *wept* on Good Friday. I prayed for good marks in exams. On Sundays I was obliged to learn the Collect by heart, and every weekday a dozen verses of the Bible; more than two mistakes and I had to stand up for lunch, tea, and dinner. However, I could not swallow all the dogma placed before me. The idea of eating the body and drinking the blood of Jesus struck me as repulsive. I could not believe in the Creation, the

Virgin Birth, the Ascension, Heaven, Hell, or the Holy Ghost. Today I live in a Catholic country. I see my rich neighbors pay the parish priest to celebrate masses for the souls of their dear departed, and wonder about the souls of the poor. I see my rich friends buy annulments from the Vatican, a luxury beyond the reach of the poor. And I hear the clergy preach doctrines which they do not believe.

The horror of life at St. Cyprian's has been described by George Orwell, Cyril Connolly, Cecil Beaton, Gavin Maxwell, and other alumni. The horror was Mrs. Wilkes, the headmaster's wife. This satanic woman carried the art of castration to extraordinary perfection. Like a chess master playing simultaneous games against several opponents, Mrs. Wilkes played games of emotional cat-and-mouse against every boy in the school. Each of us was alternately *in favor* and *out of favor*, like the courtiers at Versailles. Cyril Connolly kept a chart in which, week by week, he graphed his position at her court. Boys who were lucky enough to have rich or aristocratic fathers were always in favor, which meant that Mrs. Wilkes showered them with privilege and affection. But boys whose fathers, like mine, were neither aristocratic nor rich were always out of favor; for four years I lived in a black cloud of rejection.

Mrs. Wilkes made such exorbitant profits out of

educating ninety boys that she was able to rent grouse-moors in Scotland during the summer and send her sons to Eton. She achieved this wealth by starving the boys. She and her husband never ate our food, but those who were privileged to sit next to Mr. Wilkes at meals pinched food off the plate of that absentminded and henpecked man. The rest of us had to supplement our diet of burnt, tepid, lumpy porridge and slimy galantine by spending our pocket money on extra food. One day Mrs. Wilkes refused to let me buy a peach. "How *dare* you?" she shouted, loud enough for the whole school to hear. "Your father is so poor that we are obliged to keep you here for almost nothing. *What right has the son of a pauper to spend money on luxuries like peaches?*"

Ten years before, George Orwell had heard Mrs. Wilkes take another charity boy apart. "Do you think that's the sort of thing a boy like you should buy? You know you're not going to grow up with money, don't you? Your people aren't rich. Don't get above yourself."

On our birthdays we were allowed to buy enormous iced cakes, and to make a ceremony of presenting the candles to the boys we liked best. But my parents could not afford the price of a cake; nor could they afford a single visit to St. Cyprian's during the four years I was there, although they lived less than fifty miles away. They had no car.

I was wretchedly homesick and was only happy when the postman brought a letter from my family; to this day, the arrival of mail excites me beyond reason. At night I went to sleep sucking on a tiny hole in a can of Nestlé's condensed milk; it tastes like mother's milk. When that ran out, I sent for free samples of toothpaste and sucked it out of the tubes. I read the *Times* and *The New Statesman* and was too worldly to make easy friends with other boys. Mr. Wilkes reported to my father, "David possesses a large fund of general information and is very grown-up in his conversation—he seems to take a serious view of life."

The richest of the fathers was Perkins Bull, an eccentric Canadian tycoon. I saw him climb onto the stage at the end of the annual school play and, to thunderous applause, hang a pearl necklace round Mrs. Wilkes's neck. The play that night was *The Comedy of Errors*, and I was cast as the Abbess. While Mrs. Wilkes was adjusting my robes in the wings, she made me rehearse, for the final time, my opening speech: "Be quiet, people. Wherefore throng you hither?" When I emphasized the wrong word, she took me by the cheek and flung me to the ground. Hardly the way to treat an Abbess—or, for that matter, a child of eleven about to face the footlights for the first time.

I started Latin at eight, and Greek at eleven. Mr. Wilkes reported to my parents, "He has a distinctly original mind, and is inclined to argue with his teachers that he is right and the books are wrong." Mrs. Wilkes taught history, and her methods were diabolical. "Oggilvy"—she enjoyed mispronouncing the names of the boys who were out of favor—"what nationality was Napoleon?" Obviously a trap. If Napoleon had been French, she would not ask. I remembered that his brother Louis had been King of Holland. "Dutch?" For this gaffe she sent me to bed without supper. This malevolent matriarch remained the central figure in my nightmares until after I grew up.

My best friend at St. Cyprian's was Johnnie Rotherham, a taciturn, phlegmatic boy who is now an air vice-marshal. My happiest vacations were spent staying with his family in Warwickshire. His mother bubbled with perpetual gaiety, his father was the funniest grownup I ever encountered, and his sister Jean was the most adorable girl in the world. Johnnie taught me to shoot and to ride, and took me cubbing. If I am allowed to choose the scene to recapture on my deathbed, it will be set in the home of that happy family.

I spent only brief interludes at home with my parents, who had moved to Guildford. Poor as they were, they employed a maid, a spooky old prune who had worked in the house when it belonged to Lewis Carroll, whose real name was Dodgson. One day during luncheon she stared at me transfixed. "I see Mr. Dodgson! There he is, *in your chair!*" Not long afterward an old lady called Mrs. Hargreaves came to tea; her maiden name had been Alice Liddell, and she was the original Alice in Wonderland. Left to ourselves, we children played Kikkipegs, Sardines, Attaque, Halfpenny Nap, Dumb Crambo, and Racing Demon, and fought like the cats of Kilkenny about the pronunciation of Latin.

I came to resent my parents' poverty, may God forgive me, and cadged for invitations to visit our rich relations. At Uncle Beresford Heaton's house there were Turners in the drawing room, cigars in the smoking room, cream on the apple pie, hunters in the stables, and a garden full of gardeners. Uncle Beresford was a messy eater. During a formal dinner party, his head parlormaid earned the gratitude of his family by blurting out, "Sir, you are disgusting."

My chief hero was my Scottish grandfather, Frank Ogilvy. Where my father was warmhearted, affectionate, and a failure, Grandfather was cold-hearted, formidable, and successful. I think he was cold-hearted because his mother had thrashed him when he was four years old, and died the next day; it was his only memory of her. The son of an impecunious Scottish laird, he had left school at fourteen and joined Ogilvy Gillanders, the family firm in Liverpool. He married young, and emigrated to the Argentine, where he managed an estancia for a group of Scottish investors and fought in the Argentine army against Paraguay. When the estancia failed, Grandfather found himself out of work, with a large family to support. After prospecting for gold in New Zealand, and finding none, he went to London and got a job as secretary in the English Bank of Rio de Janeiro. Four years later, this uneducated sheep farmer became manager of Brown Shipley, where he trained Montagu Norman, the future governor of the Bank of England. He was able to send all seven of his children to private schools and universities. Grandfather lived like a Forsyte. I was impressed by the candy sugar he put in his Turkish coffee; by his cigarettes which came from Brazil and were made of black tobacco; and by his habit of using a knife and fork to peel pears and apples at the dinner table. When I told him that I had just returned from Marseilles and pronounced it *à la française*, he snorted, "You would not say *Paree*, would you? In English conversation one says *Marsails*." When I was ten, he was gratified to detect in me signs of his own acumen, as when I overheard one of my schoolmasters say that he had it in mind to confiscate the rubber balls which the boys had been collecting; I sold my collection before the news broke.

When my father appealed to Grandfather to

lend him some money and Grandfather refused, my father tried to commit suicide by cutting his throat. Grandfather told me, "The trouble with your father is that he is too thin-skinned." From that time on, my parents lived on an income of less than $1,000 a year.

Perceiving that I was bitten with ambition, Grandfather advised me to take dancing lessons. "If you can dance with your boss's wife better than he can, fortune will smile on you." He gave me other valuable advice: "When you grow up and go out into the world, you will probably find your way to New York. I advise you to study the methods of J. P. Morgan & Company. There is no other institution quite like it." Twenty-five years later I duly went to New York and studied J. P. Morgan & Company. Mr. Morgan described his partners as gentlemen with brains, and I made that my touchstone in selecting partners for Ogilvy & Mather. He also said that his bank must always confine itself to "First Class business, and that in a First Class way." This too became my policy at Ogilvy & Mather.

Grandfather had been a cricketer, and belonged to the Marylebone Cricket Club, which is to cricket what the Royal and Ancient at St. Andrews is to golf. It was paradise to sit with him on the top of the pavilion at Lords—until Frank Mann, the gigantic captain of Middlesex, started bombarding the pavilion off the slow bowling of J. C. White of Somerset. I was so frightened that I took refuge in the lavatory. "You are very leaky today," said Grandfather. My own career as a cricketer was cut short when a fast ball hit me in the groin. If it had not been for this accident, I might have begotten ten children instead of one.

During the Franco-Prussian war, Grandfather's brother David Ogilvy enlisted in the French Army and was appointed to the staff of the 18th Corps d'Armée. Paris was under siege, and the Prussians were near Orléans. Uncle David had a plan which, he thought, might save France. He found the government in Tours and contrived to present his plan to Gambetta, the Minister of War. Gambetta endorsed it, and sent him to see General Crouzat at Gien. Uncle David impressed Crouzat as *fort intelligent, fort instruit, fort distingué et qui aimait bien la France.* Riding back from Gien, Uncle David stumbled into a skirmish outside Ladon and was killed. They buried him in the village church; a stained-glass window shows him expiring in the arms of a French comrade. His widow was given a pension by the French government and survived him for sixty-eight years. She drove Grandfather up the wall. "Your Aunt Evelyn is welcome to believe in the afterlife if she chooses to do so, but she has no right to assume that I share her belief. I have had a long innings. I have had two wonderful wives, I am ninety-one, and I am ready to go." The following year he went.

When I was thirteen, I got a scholarship at Fettes, a boarding school on the outskirts of Edinburgh. Instead of disgusting St. Cyprian's porridge, Fettes provided delicious Scottish porridge, three times a day, and Scottish roast beef, and Scottish mutton pies. For the next five years I lived like a fighting cock.

Fettes was in my blood. It had been shaped by my great-uncle Lord Inglis of Glencorse, the advocate who defended Madeleine Smith when she was tried for poisoning her lover. My father and my brother had both been classical scholars at Fettes, and both had played rugby for the school. I was determined to follow their example, but asthma robbed me of stamina on the football field, and I was bored by Latin, except when it was mixed up with English in macaronic carols like "In Dulci Jubilo":

> *Ubi sunt gaudia*
> *In any place but there?*
> *There are angels singing*
> *Nova cantica*
> *And there the bells are ringing*
> *In regis curia*
> *O that we were there.*

The most agreeable of all Latin is found in this
boisterous song by John O'Keeffe (1747–1833):

Amo, amas, I love a lass,
As a cedar tall and slender;
   Sweet Cowslip's grace
   Is her nominative case,
And she's of the feminine gender.

Rorum, corum, sunt Divorum,
Harum scarum Divo!
Tag rag, merry derry, periwig and hatband!
Hic, hoc, horum, Genitivo!

If you like Vergil and Cicero better than that, I
pity you.

I was allowed to give up Latin and Greek in
favor of modern history. A curious aspect of
British education in those days was the total absence of American history from the curriculum.
My history master Walter Sellar summed up the
prevailing attitude in his comic *1066 and All That.*
After the American Revolution, he wrote, "The
Americans made Wittington President and gave
up speaking English and became USA and Columbia and 100%, etc. This was a Good Thing in
the end, as it was a cause of the British Empire,
but it prevented America from having any more
History."

I would have found the study of history more

24

interesting if I had been allowed to read memoirs and biographies instead of tedious textbooks by Sir Charles Oman and windy essays by Lord Acton. I remember only one sentence from all the history I read at Fettes. It occurs in Sir Archibald Allison's *History of Europe:* "The Austrians held the Po while the Italians slowly evacuated."

When I arrived at Fettes I had the good fortune to be put in a boarding house reserved for boys who paid no fees; their fathers were clergymen or schoolmasters, so they had grown up in a more bookish atmosphere than the other boys. Our house was an island of civilization in an ocean of philistia. We new boys were bullied unmercifully, but I was able to stop this by persuading my fellow victims to join me in ostracizing the ringleader of the bullies. Every time he came into the room, we fell silent and turned our backs; within three weeks he had a nervous breakdown.

When we broke rules, we were flogged by the masters or the prefects. One day the master who taught French reported me to my housemaster for being inattentive, and I was summoned for execution. I was aware that my housemaster detested the French master. "Sir," I said, "if the boys in Mr. Rhoades's class are not attentive, it is nobody's fault but his own." "I am bound to confess that I agree with you," he replied. When I became a prefect, I refused to take part in the floggings; in this I was supported by Hal Summers, a scholar and musician who was to become head of the Department of the Environment in London.

Alas, I was no musician. During one vacation I lay in the bath belting out Psalm 104—"There go the ships and there is that Leviathan." At the Amen, my father let out a cheer from the next room. "Why did you cheer?" I asked at breakfast. "Because," he replied, "that was the first time I have ever heard you sing anything without changing key in the middle." He timed his eggs by whistling the overture to *Figaro* while they were boiling; four minutes.

I can listen to symphonies in my mind's ear, with all the color of orchestration, but from my mother I inherited a heartbreaking inability to make the proper sounds come out of my mouth. However, I learned to play the double-bass well enough to play in the school orchestra. The bass has one advantage: it plays an octave below the cello, with the result that few conductors can hear whether you are playing in tune. But it is a *dangerous* instrument. During my first concert I was knocked almost insensible by a blow behind my left ear. I thought the tympanist had thrown his music stand at my head. My E-string had snapped with the force of a ship's hawser. To press the huge strings onto the fingerboard required stronger fingers than mine; heaven knows how

Miss Orin O'Brien, the beautiful bass player in the New York Philharmonic, can do it. The best double-bass who ever lived was Dragonetti. His dog always sat beside him in the orchestra. Beethoven took fiendish pleasure in trying to write bass parts which would be too difficult for his friend Dragonetti to play; I came to hate Dragonetti. Under full power, a double-bass makes the floorboards vibrate, which tickles your foot and makes it difficult to preserve your composure. It is the *heaviest* of instruments to lug around, and unwieldy to transport from one concert hall to another. On English trains it used to be carried at the same rate as tricyles. Cellos traveled as sewing machines.

I made money betting that I could play the D below the E of the lowest string. The trick is to put a lot of rosin on your bow and drag it across the *tailpiece*. Out comes D. Henry Havergal, the splendid music master at Fettes, took me to the Three Choirs Festival in Gloucester Cathedral. There I rubbed shoulders with Bernard Shaw, Elgar, Vaughan Williams, and Dame Ethel Smyth. Elgar wore a dove-gray frock coat and an orchid in his buttonhole. Vaughan Williams looked like a benign elephant. Dame Ethel wore a Chinese mandarin coat of ineffable distinction.

When I became a director of the New York Philharmonic in 1960, the orchestra had fallen on evil days. The critics were panning the performances, the morale of the musicians was depressed, and the concerts were half empty. When it was proposed that we engage Leonard Bernstein as head conductor, the other directors cheered. "No doubt he is great box office," I said. "He will sell a lot of tickets. But he has such a genius for personal publicity that in five years the Philharmonic will be known as Bernstein's Band." Said old Mrs. Steinway, "That's what everybody told me when we made Mahler our conductor in 1909." Well, Bernstein was a howling success, the Philharmonic recovered, and five years later the music critic of the *New York Times* referred to it as Bernstein's Band.

The other Philharmonic directors had been chosen because they were very rich, or very musical, or both. Being neither, I cast myself in the role of house bolshevik. At my first board meeting we were told that one of the violinists had died after thirty-five years with the orchestra, leaving his widow in poverty. Would the board grant her an *ex gratia* pension? I was the only director who voted in favor; I have always been shocked by the flinty hearts of people who have never known poverty.

In those days the musicians in American orchestras were paid $5,000 a year—less than plumbers and carpenters—and I always sympathized with their union during labor negotiations. But things have changed. Today, the musicians are paid such high salaries that all orchestras are threatened with bankruptcy. It is largely the fault of the nineteenth-century composers who scored their music for gigantic orchetras, culminating in Mahler's Symphony of a Thousand. Bach, Handel, and Haydn composed for orchestras of less than thirty; modern orchestras are obliged to field more than a hundred at every concert. At $25,000 a year per musician, the bill is unbearable. On top of that, the conductors pull down $100,000 a year, some of the soloists get $12,000 per engagement, and a good choir charges $12,000 to sing an oratorio. Pity the poor beggars who have to raise funds to pay these bills.

Why do conductors live so long? Toscanini, Bruno Walter, Mengelberg, Damrosch, Klemperer, Ansermet, Monteux, Casals, Adrian Boult, Beecham, and Stokowski were all conducting in their eighties. Dr. Leonard Gordon and Dr. Jerome Z. Litt have suggested that it is because they continue to take violent exercise long after other men have become inactive. Or could it be that rapturous applause, week after week, makes life worth prolonging? The first time I met Walter Damrosch, he went to the piano and performed what he called "God Save the King *With Gunfire*." This consisted of playing the music with his hands, and producing the cannonade by bumping his bottom rhythmically on the bass.

Have you noticed that people who like music seldom like poetry, and vice versa? Poetry leaves me stone cold, except for schoolboy stuff like Kipling and Newbolt. The only poet I have ever met was Yeats; I stood beside him in the pissoir the night I joined the Savile Club. He was then seventy, rejuvenated with monkey glands. I was full of claret—a bottle recommended by the old wine waiter, who recalled that it had been Robert Louis Stevenson's favorite when he was a member.

I have an Englishman's passion for oratorio, sacred and profane. *Elijah* which Mendelssohn himself thought too sugary, has me in happy tears throughout. Anything by Lully, Rameau, or Couperin is guaranteed to pull me out of the deepest sulk, and the heroic arias of Handel, with trumpet obbligato, send me into transports. Notably "Sound an Alarm" in *Judas Maccabaeus*, "Revenge Timotheus Cries" in *Alexander's Feast*, "The Trumpet Shall Sound" in *Messiah*, and "Let the Bright Seraphim" for soprano and high trumpet. I cannot bear Chopin, Wagner, Verdi, or Puccini, but I am never happier than listening to Mozart. I drive my wife mad by playing military marches on the gramophone. Jazz and its derivations are above my head; the only dances I like are polkas and hornpipes. Of all symphonies I give the prize to Beethoven's preposterous Battle Symphony (Opus 91), composed in honor of Wellington's victory over Joseph Bonaparte at Vitoria in 1813. In case you have never heard it—and few people have—*it is scored for three mechanical orchestras and an arsenal of muskets, howitzers, and cannons.* It opens with "Rule Britannia" and closes with "God Save the King." What more can you ask?

Back to school days at Fettes. I was too odd to be popular, but I made a few golden friendships. Best of all was Alastair Sharp, who arrived at Fettes with such a strong Aberdeen accent that I could not understand what he said. He was a remarkable violinist and led the school orchestra when he was twelve. "Now he is a judge—and a good judge too." Then there was Knox Cunningham, a tall and boisterous Irishman who was captain of football. When Knox discovered that I shared his passion for Synge, Lady Gregory, and Sean O'Casey, he put me in the Second XV, an honor which carried many privileges with it. Thirty years later, when he was parliamentary private secretary to the Prime Minister, I asked him for another act of patronage—a safe seat in Parliament. He thought I was drunk.

Another Irish boy, Bryan Wingfield of Powerscourt, used to fold his hands in prayer while sitting in his corner before boxing fights. He was the only boy who died while I was at Fettes. Illness was discouraged. If you could persuade the doctor to send you to the school infirmary, you were dragged there in a sort of rickshaw, called the Death Cart. On arrival the matron handed you a beaker of castor oil, with no regard for the nature of your illness. However, when I was admitted with rheumatic fever, this dear dragon saved my life by her gentle nursing. She had known my grandmother in Inverness during the seventies and remembered seeing her arrive at the Highland Ball in the family wheelbarrow, her crinoline being too big for a brougham.

The younger boys were employed as "fags" to the prefects, cleaning their rooms, polishing their shoes and cooking their suppers. At this I excelled, because I had been brought up to do such chores at home. On Sundays we were obliged to go to church in Edinburgh, trudging through the streets in top hats and tailcoats to Holy Trinity, which was Episcopalian, or St. Stephens, which was Presbyterian. Being a refugee from England, I chose Trinity, but later switched to St. Stephens. A solicitous master inferred that I must be going through a period of religious torment, and volunteered to counsel me. I did not confess my real motive, which was that the walk to St. Stephens was shorter. I found the Presbyterian church as tedious as it was hideous, and was revolted by the metrical psalms.

On top of that there were thirteen services a week in the school chapel, and attendance was compulsory. The choir always sang *fortissimo*, and the visiting preachers were inspiring—notably George Macleod, Harry Miller, and Dr. Waugh, the Dean of the Thistle. Their sermons exorcised the poisonous values I had acquired at St. Cyprian's. From that day to this I have never heard a preacher who could hold a candle to them.

Once a month there were lectures by distinguished visitors who appeared to be selected for their irresistibly funny speech defects. I cannot forget the retired admiral who lectured us on the battle of Zeebrugge. The climax came when, with a stentorian belch, he shouted: "At this point, Bonham-Carter *blew his bottom out!*"

During the vacations I fell in love with pretty girls, but a few weeks after returning to the monastic life at Fettes, transferred my affections to members of my own sex, like the inmate of a prison. Forty years later, in 1968, I returned to Fettes and delivered the oration on Founder's Day:

I have been reading the will of our Founder. He left his estate "for the maintenance, education and outfit of young people whose parents are unable to give suitable education to their children." What right had the first Governors to decide that our Founder meant

33

only *boy* children? He clearly intended that this great school should educate girls as well as boys. If the Governors continue to ignore his wishes, I urge you boys to follow the example of your contemporaries at foreign universities—*riot!*

This was greeted with loud and prolonged applause from the boys, and the following year Fettes went co-ed. I went on to sympathize with the boys for the tyranny of examinations:

The masters cram you full of facts, so that you can pass examinations. This is like cramming corn down the throat of a goose to enlarge his liver. It may produce excellent *pâté de foie gras*, but it does the goose no permanent good. The mission of a great school should not be to cram you with facts so that you can regurgitate them a few weeks later at an exam, but to inspire you with a taste for scholarship which will last you *all your life.*

Then I tried to comfort the majority who, like me, failed to become big shots at school:

I wasn't a scholar. I was a duffer at games. I detested the philistines who ruled the roost. I was a rebel and a misfit. In short, a *dud.* Fellow duds, take heart! There is no correlation between success at school and success in life. Consider my friend Iain Macleod—historian, Minister of Health, Minister of Labour, Secretary of State for the Colonies, Leader of the House of Commons. Iain was a dud at Fettes. Another dud had only one claim to fame at school—his nickname was Dung-Pat. By the time I knew him, Dung-Pat had become Governor of the Hudson's Bay Company and High Sheriff of London.

I assumed that I would never be asked to speak at Fettes again, but six years later I was invited to address the Commemoration dinner:

The survival of all private schools is in question. They are threatened by inflation, taxation, and the hostility of left-wing governments. If Fettes is to survive, it must have a *reason* to survive. It must be *different*. I suggest that you make Fettes a temple of gastronomy. If you hire a great French chef, Fettes will become known as the school where the cooking is superlative—three stars. I would train all Fettesians to be plumbers, carpenters, electricians, painters, and gardeners, thereby emancipating them from dependence on tradesmen whose services they will never be able to afford. I would make attendance at all classes optional, and make the boys *pay* to enter the classroom, like buying a ticket to the movies. This would enrich the masters who teach well, and starve the bores. I would motivate the boys to work hard by paying them a cash bonus for high marks. If I had been paid during my education, I would now be Regius Professor of History at Oxford.

When I was seventeen, I applied for the job of advertising manager at Liberty's, the fabric shop in London. Nothing doing. A few weeks later a famous but unhinged surgeon dazzled his students by performing an esoteric operation on my sphenoidal sinus, and did it so badly that my mastoid process became infected. I was not alone in believing that I was about to die. My life was saved by another surgeon, but the infection did not clear up, and three months later I was subjected to a third operation. I shall never forget my relief when the surgeon broke the news that I would never be able to play rugby football again.

I then wrote my first advertisement: YOUNG MAN SEEKS JOB AS MALE SECRETARY AND TRAVELLING COMPANION. This innocent lollipop appeared in the Continental edition of the *Daily Mail*, and pulled a reply from an American in Paris, by name Morton. Would I send my photograph? That did the trick and ten days later his chauffeur met me at the Gare du Nord. Mr. Morton apologized for putting me in a separate room, but he had a bad cold. His room stank of scent and parrot droppings. The next morning we went motoring. Where would I like to travel? China? South America? What could he buy me at Hermes? Would I like to hear Bruno Walter conduct a Russian choir? None of this struck me as in any way peculiar, but after dinner that night he announced that his cold was better, so I could sleep with him. I bolted my door and ignored the stream of invective which he hurled over the transom. Early the next morning I escaped to London and took a taxi to Grandfather's house. "I don't know why you should be surprised," he said. "We all know there are men like that in the world. If you take my advice, you will pipe down and say no more about it."

The following summer a rich American was looking for someone to tutor his illegitimate son, and required the following qualifications:

> *teach piano*
> *teach painting*
> *drive a car*
> *play tennis as a professional*

I could do none of these things, but said I could do them all. He lived in Ville-d'Avray, Corot's stamping ground near Versailles. Two days after I arrived, he took me to dine in an expensive restaurant. After brandy and cigars, he looked at me sideways. "I have to ask you an embarrassing question," he said. "The fact is, I have a *mistress*. I was afraid this would shock you, so I sent her away. But I miss her dreadfully. What would you say if Marcelle came back tomorrow?"

Marcelle was a delicious midinette, and she took a fancy to me. "*Monsieur B me fait de l'amour dans les bois, et il le fait comme un* chien!" Would I like to do it in bed? When I suggested that this would be disloyal to our employer, she told him that I had tried to seduce her, and I was banished to Brittany with the son. The poor little bastard quickly discovered that I could neither paint nor play the piano, and threatened to denounce me to his father as an impostor. This made me ill enough to take sanctuary in the American Hospital in Paris. There I shared a room with Frank Scully, a one-legged journalist from Los Angeles. Scully read aloud to me a book he was ghosting for Frank Harris about Bernard Shaw and Ellen Terry. Every afternoon we were visited by Scully's friend Anita Loos, she of the huge eyes and deep bass voice who wrote *Gentlemen Prefer Blondes*.

I decided to apply for a scholarship at a university, and chose Oxford, thereby avoiding competition with my father, my brother Francis, and the rest of my family, who had all distinguished themselves at Cambridge. But I could not afford

Oxford unless I won a scholarship, and this would not be easy; there were very few of them and they were awarded on the basis of academic excellence. It was arranged for Sligger Urquhart, a famous don at Balliol, the most intellectual of the Oxford colleges, to assess my chances. After an interview, he wrote a letter to my father which struck me as arrogant: "Your son has no chance at Balliol, but I can assure you that he will have no difficulty in winning a scholarship at any other college to which he chooses to apply."

I chose Christ Church, Henry VIII's magnificent foundation, because it had produced more Prime Ministers, Viceroys of India, and Archbishops of Canterbury than all the other colleges put together; it was said that when Henry VIII founded Christ Church he repressed his natural inclination to found a *woman's* college. Not long afterward I was to be seen, my head swathed in bandages from an operation, writing examination papers among a swarm of other candidates in Wolsey's great dining hall. Keith Feiling, the historian, was the chief examiner, and he was sufficiently impressed by my essay to invite me to spend the weekend at his house in the Cotswolds. "You know no history," he told me, "so we are going to give you a scholarship." I was the beneficiary of the Christ Church theory that scholarships should be given to those who showed the greatest promise for the future; it was believed that those who scored high marks in the examination were likely to be second-rate.

In addition to money, the scholarship conferred three conspicuous privileges: a specially long gown, a stall in the Cathedral, and the right to intone the Latin grace before dinner. The dons took exceptional pains to tutor me, in the expectation that I would one day become a don myself. Two future vice-chancellors, J. C. Masterman and R. B. McCallum, tried their best to teach me history, as did Patrick Gordon-Walker, a future Secretary of State for Foreign Affairs, and Nowell Myres. A. S. Russell tried to teach me chemistry, but in the examination, being my mother's son, I made the mistake of *smelling* the compound which I was asked to analyze; the smell was so powerful that it knocked me over backward and I lost consciousness. John Lorne Campbell of Canna tried to teach me Gaelic. But I was unteachable in any subject. To conclude that I was bone-idle begs the question: *why* was I bone-idle? Perhaps it was fatigue; I spent most nights propped up on pillows, struggling with asthma. But I was not too fatigued to play court tennis next morning, ride in the afternoon, and dine at John Fothergill's Spread Eagle; in his memoirs Fothergill remembered me as a "boisterous, handsome and almost idiotic great lad." Perhaps it was impatience with academe and the itch to start earning a living. Perhaps I was intellectually out of my depth. Whatever the reason, I failed every examination.

Out of two hundred and fifty graduates at Christ Church, fifty came from Eton and formed an obnoxious clique. They were not allowed motor cars, but one of them registered his Rolls-Royce in the name of his chauffeur. Another engaged Sophie Tucker to entertain his undergraduate friends at supper. Some employed grooms to look after their hunters. Some had inherited titles from their ancestors—the Duke of Wessex, the Marquis of Loamshire, the Earl of Blackpool, and so forth. As hereditary members of the House of Lords, these callow youths were entitled to legislate. It occurred to me that the easiest way to stop this racket would be for all the other undergraduates to help themselves to titles. Garter King of Arms would hemorrhage, but he would be powerless to prevent it. The House of Lords had been the target of Gilbert's ridicule fifty years before, and in 1909 Winston Churchill, himself the grandson of a duke, had written a book attacking the system that "requires that we shall maintain in our country a superior caste, with law-giving functions inherent in their blood . . . irrespective of the character, the intelligence or the experience." That "superior caste" is still exercising its law-giving function in 1977.

I have always been able to forget the unhappy periods in my life, and recall only the seven happy incidents of my two years at Oxford:

Dining at the Balliol high table as the guest of Sandy Lindsay, the great man who was then Master.

Winning twenty pounds when, on the strength of a tip from a spiritualist, I backed Orpen in the Derby.

Joining the Fellowship of St. Alban and St. Sergius, whose purpose was to bring about the union of the Anglican and Orthodox Russian churches, under the leadership of Father Bulgakov.

A boozy revel at Blenheim Palace on the sixtieth birthday of the Duke of Marlborough, organized by that brave madman General Jack Seely.

Presiding over the White Rose Society, whose fatuous purpose was to restore the Stuarts to the throne of England.

Being persuaded by Lady Astor, so seductive was her Virginian charm, to stop drinking for three weeks.

Expeditions to London to see Bailiev's Chauve-Souris, returning to Oxford on the last train, which was known as the Flying Fornicator.

Thus I frittered time away. In extenuation, I can only plead that thirty-five years later I raised a considerable sum of money for Christ Church by drafting begging letters to the American alumni. They were signed, without alteration, by Henry Luce and my dearly loved friend Cuthbert Simpson, the Dean of Christ Church.

Cuthbert told me a story. In the 1860s a bumptious young man was inveighing against Oliver Cromwell. An old woman protested, "My husband's first wife's first husband *knew* Oliver Cromwell—and liked him very much." Two hundred years.

[2]

I Become a Chef in Paris

M Y father must have been mortified by my failure to become a don, but he kept it to himself and did his best to restore my self-confidence. "I am sure you will land on your feet. You always do." But my feeling of guilt and disappointment was not to be exorcised until many years later, when a psychoanalyst observed that dons were pickled undergraduates.

I ran away from academe and became a cook at the Hotel Majestic in Paris. There I found the discipline I needed. For ten hours a day, six days a week, I had to stand ramrod straight at a red-hot stove, soaked in sweat from head to foot. Monsieur Bourgignon, the head *saucier*, told me that every chef, by the time he was forty, was either dead or crazy. The other cooks had already served their apprenticeship, so I started at the bottom. My first assignment was to prepare meals for the customers' *dogs*, and particularly the poodles of a certain countess. Those spoiled bitches would only eat hot bones, and twice a day I had to fish for them in the stockpot of the *chef potagier*, a peevish drunkard who resented my incursions and bombarded me with raw eggs. Soon I was promoted to whisking egg whites for Jourdan, the *chef pâtissier*. He looked like Emil Jannings and was the most accomplished thief in the kitchen, never going home without a chicken concealed in the dome of his homburg hat. Before he left on vacation, this droll Rabelaisian had me stuff the legs of his long underwear with the Majestic's hothouse peaches. He was the finest *pâtissier* in France and was chosen to make the sugar baskets and *petits fours glacés* for a banquet given at Versailles in honor of the King and Queen of England.

We cooks were given as much wine as we could drink, and very good wine it was, until it was discovered that the man in charge of the cellar was decanting Château Lafite into our bottles, and selling our plonk to the customers as Lafite. We were allowed to eat anything that took our fancy, provided it was not on the menu. Our favorite dish was *oeufs au beurre noir:* you heat some butter until it is very dark brown, almost black. Add some vinegar. Chop up a raw onion. Fry the eggs. Sprinkle them with the onion and some capers. Pour on the black butter.

I filched a hundred francs' worth of iced cakes every day, which made up for the fact that my wages were only 135 francs a month. The head chef had the same dessert at lunch every day: one slice of pineapple, three apricots, and a prune. Prepared by me.

We used to have violent arguments about recipes. The first court of appeal was always *Le Répertoire de la Cuisine* by Gringoire and Saulnier. If that did not settle it, we had recourse to Escoffier's immortal *Guide Culinaire*. One of the chefs had worked under Escoffier ("the King of Chefs and the Chef of Kings") at the Savoy in London and had seen him sign receipts for cartloads of beef which were then delivered to his brother Robert's sauce factory in the Tottenham Court Road. In such time-honored ways he became a rich man, and went to the Derby every year on the box of his own four-in-hand. It was a great day when he emerged from retirement and lunched with us in the Majestic kitchen; he was then eighty-five and looked like a Victorian banker.

The head chef at the Majestic was Monsieur Pitard, and a more terrifying martinet I have never encountered. He worked at a desk in the middle of the kitchen, his beady eye always upon us. One day he noticed that the tops on a batch of *brioches* were crooked, and fired the culprit on the spot. When he overheard me tell a waiter that one of the dishes on the menu was finished, he bawled me out. "A great kitchen must always honor what is on the menu."

"But, Chef," I pleaded, "it was roast chicken, and it would have taken forty minutes to roast another."

"Don't you know that you can roast a chicken in fifteen minutes if you heat the oven to six hundred degrees?"

"Suppose the *plat du jour* is *coulibiac*, which takes all day to prepare?"

"In that kind of emergency, come and tell me. I will telephone to other establishments until I find one which also has *coulibiac* on the menu. Then I will send you to fetch it in a taxi."

My next post was in the *garde-manger* where I prepared the *hors d'oeuvres*, a minimum of twenty-six different varieties for each meal. I also made the mayonnaise. The rule was to break each egg separately into a cup and smell it before adding it to the others. One morning I was in too much of a hurry to observe this precaution. The fifty-ninth egg was rotten and contaminated all the others. I had no choice but to throw the whole batch into the garbage. If Pitard had seen me, he would have fired me. That afternoon the *chef garde-manger* sent me to the *chef saucier* with some raw sweetbreads which smelled so putrid that I knew they would endanger the life of any client who ate them. I protested to the *chef garde-manger*, but he told me to carry out his order; he knew that he would be in hot water if Pitard discovered that he had run out of sweetbreads. I had been brought up to believe that it is dishonorable to inform. But I did just that. I took the putrid sweetbreads to Pitard, and invited him to smell them. Without a word, he went over to the *chef garde-manger* and fired him. The poor devil had to leave, then and there.

In those days suppliers gave head chefs princely commissions on everything they bought. Thus Pitard could afford to live in a château. He came to work in a taxi, wearing a bowler hat and carrying a gold-knobbed cane. The other cooks were miserably poor, there being no trade unions in those days. The young ones were a rough lot, except for Pascal and Pierre. Poor Pascal was an intellectual and much disliked; one night in the dressing room I saw Régis, a bad guy, evacuate his bowels into poor Pascal's new shoes. On payday the bachelors went in a party to a brothel, all except Pierre Zahnd, who was saving up to buy a concertina. Pierre was shocked by the obscene

48

language I was learning, and threatened to write to my father. I did not realize how foul-mouthed I had become until I tried to make conversation with an elderly Comtesse at a dinner party. Her blushes froze me into silence. At her house I met the exquisite Geneviève de Serrèville, then seventeen years old, and took her to her first night club —Les Matelots in Montmarte, where four long-stemmed blondes danced the can-can with more verve and prettier knickers than I have ever seen since. When Geneviève went to England, I gave her introductions that launched her in English society, but such is the stratification of French society that her father, the Baron de Serrèville, refused to receive me, a cook. Eight years later she became Sacha Guitry's fourth wife. The Comtesse introduced me to the Infanta Eulalie, the indomitable aunt of the King of Spain. Being royal, she was not a snob and applauded me for working in a kitchen—"just like my great-nephew, who is working for Mr. Ford in Detroit."

I spent my evenings at the Prado on the Avenue Wagram, where a Russian band of fourteen balalaikas made me forget that my feet ached with fatigue. When my day off fell on a Sunday, I went to the Russian church on the Rue Daru; the choir included Chaliapin, whose voice welled up from the bowels of the earth.

There were thirty-four chefs in the Majestic

brigade, and thirty-three of them were specialists
—*sauciers*, *poissoniers*, *rôtisseurs*, *potagiers*, *en-
tremêtiers*, *pâtissiers*, *glaciers*. Martin, the thirty-
fourth, was a versatile genius from La Vendée who
took charge of each department when its director was off duty. Finally, there was the *chef
trancheur*, the carver, whose station during the
service of meals was in the restaurant. He was
chosen for his good looks, and I was jealous of him.
He called me *Sauvage*, because I came from Scotland.

I lived in the garden court of a modest hotel on
the Rue Lauriston, just along from the real tennis
court. Among the other inmates was the service
manager of Rolls-Royce, through whom I got to
know the chauffeurs of the Parisian upper-crust
and heard rich gossip about their employers.
There was also an old Frenchman who had once
been Stanley Baldwin's butler—"a stupid man, a
real John Bull, that Baldwin. He speaks no language but his own." He disapproved of my working as a cook: "You ought not to work, you ought
to be a little gentleman."

A few days after I joined the Majestic brigade,
an American customer asked for mint sauce with
his mutton, and I was the only chef who knew how
to make it. I was also the only chef who knew how
to make junket. But I finally won Pitard's approval when an elderly matron who occupied

seven rooms in the hotel threatened to move out
unless her baked apples were better prepared.
She was on a diet which restricted her to one
baked apple at every meal, and demanded a bigger one than we could find in the market. My solu-
tion was to bake *two* apples, pass their flesh
through a sieve, and put both into one skin.

One night the President of France was coming
to dinner. My assignment was to remove the bones
of raw ducks without making any incisions in their
skin; this was not cooking, it was surgery. I then
had to decorate the shapely thighs of cold frogs
with chervil leaves; this was not cookery, it was
jewelry, requiring good eyesight, a steady hand,
and a sense of design. Suddenly I became aware
that Pitard was standing over me, watching in-
tently. After five minutes of ominous silence, he
signaled for the entire brigade to gather round.
La vache, I thought, he is going to fire me, and he
is going to do it in front of an audience, like a
public hanging. My hands shook and my knees
buckled, but I kept on working. When the circle
had formed, Pitard pointed to my frog's legs.
"*That*," he said, "*is the way to do it*." Later he
took me upstairs and showed me President
Doumer eating my frog's legs. A waiter handed
me a glass of champagne—*Vive le Sauvage!* On
another occasion I was allowed to watch President
Doumer consume a soufflé Rothschild (with three

liqueurs) which I had cooked. Three weeks later, he died—not from my soufflé, but from the bullet of a mad Russian.

The illustrious Henri Soulé of the Pavillon once told me that our Majestic brigade had been the best of all time. With a leader like Pitard, how could it be anything else?

In the Majestic kitchens, the floors were scrubbed and fresh sawdust put down twice a day. Twice a day I had to shave the top off the wooden table on which the raw meat was trimmed. Twice a month a Polish bug-killer came round in search of roaches. Every morning the chefs were issued clean uniforms—check trousers, white jackets, a white apron, a white neckerchief, and a starched white toque.

We looked down our noses at the *loufiats* (waiters). The only thing they had to do was take our creations upstairs and plunk them down in front of the customers. Lowest of all in the caste system were the Algerian *plongeurs*, who washed our saucepans, one hundred and fifty of them, all copper.

To become the head of a big French kitchen takes as long as to become the chief of surgery in a big hospital. You have to know a vast repertoire of dishes. You have to be able to discipline a brigade of hot-tempered lunatics. And, rare among chefs, you need sufficient education to cope with the paper work of ordering supplies and planning menus. Time and again I have seen excellent chefs invest their savings in restaurants, only to fail for lack of education.

The kitchens at the Majestic were underground, hot as the hinges of hell, and just as noisy. On my day off, I used to go by train and horse bus to La Verrière where I lay on my back in a meadow, looking at the sky and smelling the flowers. After lunch I walked for twenty miles around Les Vaux, St. Benoit, Vieille Eglise, and Rambouillet, always alone but happy as a sand-boy.

You ask whether I ever cook nowadays? The answer is yes, but rarely. I learned from the chefs at the Majestic that it is the better part of wisdom to stay out of your wife's kitchen. However, I suspect that hostesses cook their best when I am coming to dinner.

If I stayed at the Majestic, I faced fifteen years of slave wages, fiendish pressure, and perpetual exhaustion. So, when I was offered a job selling Aga cooking stoves to chefs in Britain, I took it. The Aga is the most remarkable product I have ever known. Invented by Gustaf Dalén, the Swedish physicist and Nobel Prize-winner, it is so thermally efficient that one small injection of anthracite keeps it at a constant temperature for twenty-four hours. My brother Francis had helped to launch the Aga by writing a letter to headmasters of boarding schools—in Greek; when some of the headmasters replied that they could not read Greek, Francis wrote again—in Latin. My first assignment was to teach the chefs at the Junior Constitutional Club in Piccadilly how to use their Agas. I did this without difficulty, but I could not teach those lackadaisical English chefs how to cook. Their slovenly work and lack of pride was in painful contrast to the professionalism and *esprit de corps* of the Majestic brigade. I then had the good fortune to sell Agas to Glenalmond, a Scottish boarding school very much like Fettes. One condition was attached to this lucrative order: that I teach the school cooks how to use my stoves. Before breakfast the first morning I presented myself in the kitchen, resplendent in Majestic uniform.

"What is on the menu?" I asked the steward.

"Scrambled eggs," he replied.

"How many boys?"

"Two hundred."

"Give me four hundred eggs."

"I will give you thirty, *and as much egg powder as you want.*"

I refused to have anything to do with this outrage, and half an hour later had the satisfaction of seeing the whole ersatz mess returned from the dining hall, uneaten. It was fed to the pigs on the school farm. The second morning I persuaded the steward to give me four hundred eggs. Sure enough, the boys ate the lot, and that night I gave the masters a dinner which would have done credit to Pitard himself. After three weeks of this gastronomic revolution, the steward complained that his pigs were starving.

My best prospects were the stately homes. I found that it was a mistake to approach their owners direct, because they dared not give me an order without the permission of their cooks. It worked better to start by bearding those beldams in their kitchens; once I got *their* blessing, the rest was easy. Sometimes I promised the owner of the house, "If you buy an Aga, I will get you the best cook in Scotland." If this seductive offer was refused, I would move the stupid woman's cook to a house where my offer was accepted. In this way I made many enemies, but an equal number of grateful customers.

In those days it was not unusual for big houses to employ a dozen servants. I knew a country parson who had sixteen. The pretty ones were kept out of sight in the kitchen, while the ugly ones were allowed upstairs. Servants were seldom paid more than $100 a year, so that the parson's staff cost him less than $2,000 a year.

One morning I rang the bell at the tradesman's entrance of a stately home and found the cook distraught. Her stove (not an Aga) had broken down, and Royalty was coming to luncheon. I managed to make the stove work and persuaded the cook to let me help her. I doubt whether such a meal had ever been served in the house, and the Royal congratulations were unrestrained. At luncheon in the servants' hall, the grateful cook put me on her right, and persuaded the butler to get me an appointment upstairs, where I got my order. When I left, the cook put a brace of pheasants in the boot of my car.

I had some bizarre customers, none more so than a certain Colonel Cuthbert. When a General went to inspect his regiment, the soldiers presented arms, the band played the national anthem and the gallant Colonel mounted his horse to salute. Drunk as usual, he fell off the horse on the other side, crawled on all fours under its belly and mounted again. Again he fell off on the other side; again he crawled under the horse. Round and round, while his troops struggled to maintain their composure—and the band played "God Save the King."

One fine day I sold an Aga to David Macdonald, the Roman Catholic Archbishop of St. Andrews and Edinburgh. A week after it was installed, this saintly man came to see me. Would I like introductions to all the convents in his archdiocese? For the next three months I drove about Scotland knocking on convent doors. Every mother superior was waiting for me, pen in hand, ready to sign on the dotted line. Years later I heard that the Presbyterian scum of Edinburgh had taken to stoning the Archbishop's car. So much for the Christianity of John Knox.

The cruelty of Scottish Presbyterians showed itself in an incident which had taken place not long before. One of my cousins had sent the son of his shepherd to study art at the Slade School in London. Because the boy could not speak English, it was arranged for him to lodge in the house of a doctor who spoke Gaelic. The doctor's daughter was having an affair with a married man and became pregnant. Abortions were not available in those days, so she had to find a husband in a hurry. Who better than the country bumpkin from Scotland? Seven months after they were married a son was born and the innocent shepherd's son believed that he was the father. Proud as punch, he took his wife and the baby back to Scotland, and they would have lived happily ever afterward—had not the elders of the Presbyterian Church gotten wind of what had happened. They decided that it was their Christian duty to tell the "father" that he had been deceived. The next day he sent the baby to an orphanage, and never spoke to his wife again.

I agree with Hazlitt—"the Scotch, as a nation, are particularly disagreeable. They hate every appearance of comfort themselves, and refuse it to others. Their climate, their religion, and their habits are equally averse to pleasure. Their manners are either distinguished by a fawning sycophance, that makes one sick; or by a morose, unbending callousness, that makes one shudder." Charles Lamb said: "I have been trying all my life to like Scotchmen, and am obliged to desert from the experiment in despair. . . . The tediousness of these people is certainly provoking. I wonder if they ever tire of one another." When an Ogilvy tried to defend Scotland in the presence of Samuel Johnson, he received the famous snub, "The noblest prospect which a Scotsman ever sees is the high-road that leads him to England."

The only things I liked in Scotland were my secretary and the claret. There was more good claret in Scotland than in France. It tasted of violets, old iron, and leather.

I spent my vacations in Ireland, visiting the haunts of Grandfather Fairfield in County Kerry and gossiping at Jammet's restaurant with my Dublin friends—Erskine Childers, then an account executive in an advertising agency and later President of the Republic; Marjorie Cunningham, the headmistress of Trinity school for girls; and Sean MacEntee, the finance minister. How funny and friendly they were after the dour, suspicious Scots.

During a visit to the Aga cooking school in London, the Kensington Palace cook told me that Princess Alice was in the habit of asking her friends to give her the best recipes in their cook's repertoire. The cooks resented this and deliberately put false quantities in their recipes, so that Princess Alice's cook would not be able to use them. The Princess, who is Queen Victoria's granddaughter, gave one of these sabotaged recipes to my friend the cook and ordered her to prepare it for a dinner party. She rehearsed it without success, and was at her wit's end. I was able to diagnose the sabotage, and all went well on the night. The cook was so grateful that she invited me to watch a palace dinner party through a peephole.

Back in Edinburgh, I engaged my landlady Christine Roebuck to give cooking lectures to my prospects. This remarkable woman had emigrated from the island of Skye and bluffed her way into being hired as cook in the Fifth Avenue mansion of Harry Payne Whitney. The first night, she was faced with preparing terrapin à la Maryland. She had never heard of terrapin, still less seen one. But there it was, an enormous, armor-plated turtle, alive and kicking in the corner of the scullery. A kindly English footman volunteered to kill it for her. He placed the terrapin on the edge of the kitchen table. The terrapin withdrew its head, tail, and feet into the safety of its carapace. The footman put a poker in the fire until it was red hot

59

and then applied it to the terrapin—rectally. This so surprised the turtle that it stuck out its head to see what was going on. Whereupon the footman cut off its head with a carving knife, and Mrs. Roebuck's honor was saved.

Her cooking lessons were punctuated by inflammatory harangues on Scottish nationalism, then in its infancy. Mrs. Roebuck's flat, where I lived, was on Princes Street, looking up at the Castle. My fellow lodger was Compton Mackenzie, who had arthritis and kept me awake with groans and screams. We had frequent evenings of Highland music, washed down with Mrs. Roebuck's Athol Brose, a dangerous concoction of oatmeal, honey, and malt whisky. I lived like a prince on her cooking—trout, grouse, oat cakes, Forfar bridies, haggis, raspberry tarts, and so forth. But it did not last. One evening her friend Moray Maclaren got drunk—"so drunk he'd kiss a pig," said Mrs. Roebuck—and insulted me with such venom that I packed my bags and moved to a hotel. There an elderly widow became infatuated with me, fifty years her junior. Every Sunday afternoon we played gin rummy. The poor dear was a little gaga and thought aloud, with the result that I always knew what cards she was collecting and what she thought I was collecting. In this way I was able to double the income I earned as a salesman. Beast.

Selling Agas gave me a plausible pretext for

visiting houses which interested me. Thus I was able to inspect Hopetoun, the great Adam palace near Edinburgh, Cortachy Castle, seat of the noble Ogilvys to whom I am not related, and Corrimony in Inverness, where my grandfather grew up. In our family burial ground I found the grave of a great-aunt who died in infancy, with this diabolical Presbyterian inscription: A SINNER SAVED BY FREE GRACE. On some of these incursions I was entertained by the cook in the servants' hall, and occasionally came away with an order.

I spent my evenings at a boys' club in the Edinburgh slums. The boys came from desperately poor families and started work in factories when they were thirteen. The club leader, Nunky Brown, was the greatest probation officer of all time; I marveled at his skill in keeping delinquent boys out of prison. My assignment was to coach them in dramatics. Three of our productions were entered in a drama festival, and each won the gold medal in its class. Said the adjudicator, "Whoever directed these plays is the greatest hope for the national theater movement in Scotland." Very civil.

I sold so many Agas that the company commissioned me to write a manual for the enlightenment of the other salesmen.* I sent a copy to my

---

* When the editors of *Fortune* read it thirty years later, they reported that it was probably the best sales manual of all time.

61

brother Francis at Mather & Crowther, a London advertising agency, and they hired me. There I spent the next three years. I went to concerts, and balls which lasted until dawn. I skylarked with girls, and sailed in the Solent with Nancy and Martin de Selincourt. I played the giddy-goat with Oliver Hill. I dined out, and drank much good claret with André Simon and Maurice Healy. I helped a young American radio correspondent called Edward R. Murrow entertain the first American advertising tycoon he or I had ever met, the napoleonic Hill Blackett. When Parliament was sitting I went to the House of Commons every night and listened to the debates; dare I confess that I contemplated ending my career in Downing Street?

I made friends with Professor Namier, the Polish authority on the reign of George III. "Why," I asked him, "do you always wear a black tie?" "I put it on when King Edward VII died, and I have seen no reason since to take it off." Like everybody else in London, I got to know Lady Ottoline Morrell and had tea with the pixyish James Stephens in her garden. I remember that she had a boil on her chin and covered it with satin bandage, a huge pearl pendant dangling from it.

If all this sounds frivolous, it was; I was twenty-five. But it was during this period that I acquired the habit of hard work. And, when my salary was doubled, I tasted blood.

A Chicago clipping service kept me supplied with every new advertising campaign that broke in the United States, and I copied the best of them, down to the smallest detail, for my British clients. If anyone had suggested that twelve years later I would be in New York inventing campaigns of my own, I would not have believed him. I helped the Council of German Jewry raise money for refugees from Hitler, and stopped my agency accepting Hitler's ambassador as a client by threatening to resign if they did. But I was so intolerant that my brother, who was seven years older and already a director, had to send me a rocket:

> In the determination of your attitude both to your colleagues and to your clients, may I recommend you to consider Winston Churchill's epigram on Lord Rosebery—"He would not stoop; he did not conquer." How better could he sum up that fastidiousness of the sensitive aristocrat which can be narrower and more bigoted than the prejudice of the crowd?

[3]

New York and Hollywood

M E N who have multiple careers are to be envied. Lorenzo Da Ponte, a Venetian Jew, was converted to Christianity and studied for the priesthood, but his disreputable private life forced him to leave Italy in a hurry. He went to Vienna, became the Emperor's secretary, and wrote the libretti for Mozart's three best operas. After that he ran a drug store, and then a distillery—in Manhattan. He died at the age of eighty-nine, Professor Emeritus of Italian at Columbia University.

Judah Benjamin, the Senator from Louisiana, was the brains of the Confederate government.

64

After the Civil War he escaped to London, a penniless refugee of fifty-five. When he died, nineteen years later, he had the largest practice at the English bar.

When I emigrated to the United States, my English friends thought I was nuts. Why jettison a burgeoning career and start again in a country where I did not know a solitary soul? It wasn't as if I was a starving Sicilian or a refugee from Hitler's Germany. I had drawn a First Class ticket in the lottery of life, and here I was embarking in steerage.

Why? Partly because I wanted adventure. Partly because I figured that the same effort would produce three times as much lucre in America as in little England. Partly because I wanted to prove that I could succeed on my own, without the patronage of my brother. Partly because I was inspired by the New Deal and thought that Roosevelt was handling unemployment better than Neville Chamberlain. And partly because my imagination had been fired by books I had read, starting with *Huck Finn*, going on with Willa Cather, Edith Wharton, and Sinclair Lewis, and culminating in *John Brown's Body*, Stephen Vincent Benét's narrative poem about the Civil War. I did not share the jealous antagonism which was then prevalent in England toward the United States. An elderly judge had been heard to say, "American women dress like fashion-plates, have the voices of peacocks and the manners of cooks." When I got engaged to a girl from one of the first families of Virginia, a Scottish cousin wrote, "One always supposes that all American women are like Mrs. Simpson. However, there may be some exceptions and if so, we hope your fiancée is one of them."

Luigi Lucioni, who shared my cabin, told me about an Englishman who went to New York and stayed at the Waldorf Astoria. At the beginning of dinner on his first night, Oscar, the famous headwaiter, asked him one of the riddles for which he was famous. "My father had a child. It wasn't my brother. It wasn't my sister. Who was it?" The Englishman puzzled over this all through dinner, and finally gave up. "It was me," said Oscar. Three weeks later the Englishman was back in London and inflicted the same riddle on a dinner party. Nobody could guess the answer. "It was Oscar, the headwaiter at the Waldorf Astoria."

When the skyscrapers of Manhattan came in sight, I wept with exaltation. While the ship was being warped into the dock I could see a laborer digging up the street with a jackhammer; he was smoking a cigar, a luxury which only Dukes could afford in England.

I carried two letters of introduction. One was from Sir Humphry Rolleston, my doctor uncle,

66

to Dr. Emanuel Libman. The first time I entered Libman's office, he seized me by the neck and jabbed his thumb under my ear. It hurt like hell, and I let out a bellow. It was his invariable opening gambit; it measured the patient's threshold of pain, which he thought was an important preliminary to diagnosis. Then he stared at me in silence for several minutes.

"You have bleeding from the bowel."

"How do you know?"

"The muscles at the top of your back ache."

"How do you know?"

"Never mind how I know. Before you go to bed tonight, take six calomel. Tomorrow morning, drink a bottle of Pluto water, and follow that with an enema. Now come and lunch at Voisin—I will introduce you to Belle de Acosta Green, Mr. Morgan's librarian."

Dr. Alexis Carrel, who was then head of the Rockefeller Institute of Medical Research, told me that the most important thing in medicine was to persuade Libman to write down his methods of diagnosis before he died. But this tiny, white-faced old man got childish pleasure out of mystifying his fellow doctors and never did so. He published more than a hundred papers, but held back his magic tricks. He could *smell* disease. Once on entering a hospital ward he announced, "I smell typhoid—get him out of here." Sure

67

enough, it was found that a patient who had just been admitted was in the early stages of typhoid.

The day after Libman saw President Harding at a reception, he telephoned Eugene Meyer in Washington:

"Who is the Vice-President?" Libman asked.

"His name is Coolidge. Why do you ask?"

"Because Harding will be dead in six months."

And so he was. In 1944 Libman saw Roosevelt in a newsreel and predicted his early death of cerebral hemorrhage. One evening I ran into him at the Waldorf Astoria, where he had been the guest of honor at the graduation dinner of a great medical school. "What was your speech about?" I asked. "I did not make a speech," he replied. "I entertained them by telling each of the graduating students what he would die of."

Libman's patients included Sarah Bernhardt and Albert Einstein. When Einstein was living in Berlin, he used to cable Libman every time he felt ill, describing his symptoms. Libman sent his diagnosis by return cable. He told me that the first time Harpo Marx consulted him, he walked in *on his hands*. "Why are you walking upside down?" asked Libman. "I have diarrhea. I can't hold my stool."

Libman used most of his income, plus large sums he begged from rich patients, to subsidize the research of young doctors. When my uncle

Humphry died, Libman wrote me: "I would like to ask you to deliver the enclosed letter to Lord Moran at the Royal College of Physicians. I am giving $10,000 for a lectureship to be named for Sir Humphry Rolleston. Try me soon for dinner."

He shared a brownstone on Sixty-fourth Street with his sister, but they lived on separate floors and seldom met. One afternoon I saw an elderly man emerge from Libman's office. The gramophone was playing the Dead March from *Saul*. I asked Libman why he was playing that funereal music. "The man is dying." For many years Libman suffered sinus pain and walked about his office with a probe wrapped in cotton, sticking out of his nostril. After one of his patients died during an operation for appendicitis, he asked permission to remove the thyroid from the body. The family refused. Late that night Libman and Carrel were returning home from a dinner party and stopped by the morgue. Without a word to anybody, Libman took off his dinner jacket, inserted his arm through the appendix incision, and worked his hand all the way up, pus oozing onto his boiled shirt, until he reached the thyroid, which he removed with his fingers.

Would you like to know what I think about American cooking? The apple pie and the bread are the worst in the world. The steaks and the roast beef are the best. So is the lobster. The hams from Virginia and Tennessee are in a class by themselves—far better than hams from Bayonne or York or anywhere else in Europe. The popovers, flapjacks, and maple syrup are irresistible. The ice cream is supreme. *But that's all there is.*

The best cooks in the world are the French, the Belgians, and the Chinese. The Irish are the worst.

My other letter of introduction was from my cousin Rebecca West to Alexander Woollcott, who had been for many years the most influential drama critic in New York—fat, kind, witty, sentimental, and rude. In *Myself Among Others*, Ruth Gordon recalls my arrival on Woollcott's island in Vermont:

> Bull's motorboat hit the dock and a tall young man with flaming red hair got out and followed his luggage up the path to the breakfast table.
>
> "Livingstone, I presume," said Woollcott and turned to the table. "This is David Ogilvy. David, these are spongers."
>
> "Good morning," said the new guest, "is there a writing table?"
>
> "What kind of goddam unnatural question is *that?*" asked Woollcott. "Sit down and drink some coffee, better than you or any subject of your government deserves."

"Thanks, but first I must write the President of the Central of Vermont railroad about that *disgraceful* trip."

Woollcott's interest was caught. "What disgraceful trip was that?"

"This country must *do* something about that railroad bed. May I have a sheet of paper? I wish to register my complaint."

The "spongers" were Harpo and Susan Marx, George and Bea Kaufman, Alice Duer Miller, Raoul Fleischmann, Robert Sherwood, Ethel Barrymore, and Ruth Gordon—with whom Woollcott pretended to be in love. During a lull in the conversation at dinner, Woollcott said in a loud voice, "Ogilvy, you are a middle-class Scotsman with no talent." I spent the rest of the evening rowing Miss Barrymore on the lake in the moonlight. She told me that Churchill had fallen in love with her when she first appeared on the London stage in *Captain Jinx of the Horse Marines;* every time he had come to New York during the subsequent fifty years he had sent her roses within half an hour of landing.

I find it difficult to describe my early days in New York without gushing about American hospitality. At the top of my list I put Charles C. Burlingham, then eighty and the doyen of the reform movement. "C.C." had been responsible for exposing the corruption of Mayor Jimmy Walker

71

and had then engineered the election of Fiorello
LaGuardia. Every Sunday morning the grateful
LaGuardia typed a long letter to Burlingham re-
porting the political events of the previous week,
and I was allowed to read these masterpieces of
indiscretion. His pet hate was Mussolini, but he
kept quiet about it for fear of alienating the
Italian vote in New York. However, one evening* after a dinner at the Century, he let his
hair down to me: "Do you know what I would do
if I were Roosevelt? I would send the Atlantic
Fleet into the Mediterranean. Then I would invite
the British Navy to join in celebrating some anniversary—any anniversary would do. Then I would
anchor the combined fleets off Rome, and I would
send a signal to Mussolini: SEE HERE YOU SON OF
A BITCH, YOU LAY OFF OR GET BLOWN TO HELL!"
By this time the Little Flower was shaking his fist,
purple with rage. Burlingham taught me to play
croquet in his garden at Black Point on the Connecticut coast, and gave me an education in American politics. He lived to be a hundred, an iconoclast
to the end.

Then there were Caroline Ruutz-Rees, who had
founded Rosemary Hall girls' school in 1890; a
most *worldly* schoolmistress. Gay and Tom Fin-
letter, who became Secretary of the Air Force.
Tom Lamont, who had been a partner in J. P.
Morgan since 1911—I ate my first Thanksgiving

* October 17, 1938.

dinner under his roof. Jack Elliott and his beautiful suffragette wife Audrey, who introduced me to Robert Moses and Al Smith; one of the Elliotts' sons, then a schoolboy of fourteen, was to succeed me as chairman of Ogilvy & Mather. And finally Frances Perkins, the perennial Secretary of Labor; she gave me a work permit.

At this point I had the luckiest break of my life: Dr. George Gallup invited me to join his organization in Princeton. If you ever decide to seek your fortune in a foreign country, the best thing you can do is to get a job with the local Gallup Poll. It will teach you what the natives want out of life, what they think about the main issues of the day, what their habits are. You will quickly get to know more about the country of your adoption than most of its inhabitants. How many Americans, for example, would guess that 65 percent of their fellow countrymen say grace before meals, or that 46 percent go to church on an average Sunday? (In England it is three percent.)

George Gallup is a great man. The son of an itinerant philosopher, he escaped from poverty by keeping a herd of dairy cows when he was still in high school. At the University of Iowa he became editor of the student magazine, converted it into a daily newspaper, and invented a method for measuring the number of people who read every news item and every feature—an invention which was to revolutionize journalism and advertising. In the Presidential election of 1936, the *Literary Digest* predicted the victory of Landon by nineteen points. Gallup questioned their reliance on telephone interviews, because telephones were then confined to the upper-income groups. He polled a more representative sample of the population, and predicted the election of Roosevelt. The result was oblivion for the *Literary Digest*, renown for Gallup.

During a visit to Hollywood I had written to my brother: "I would like to apply Gallup's methods to measuring the popularity of movie stars, pretesting stories, forecasting trends, etc. The motion picture industry is threshing about in ignorance of what the public really likes. I swear it is possible to eliminate the blind ignorance and false statistics which are throttling this giant industry." By an extraordinary coincidence, this was precisely the job Gallup now asked me to do. After a few weeks of indoctrination, I accompanied him to Hollywood, armed with a letter from Henry Sell of liver *pâté* fame to Constance Bennett: "A very beautiful and rich young Englishman is on his way to Hollywood.* He's definitely not the regular run of Englishman but more the Evelyn Waugh hero type." The day we

* I had $400 in the world.

74

arrived, Gallup and I lunched with George Schaefer, head of the RKO studios. Gallup was no salesman, and I was tongue-tied with nerves, until Schaefer reached under the table and snapped the elastic in my Congress gaiters. This unfroze me, and I was able to put on an articulate pitch. We then drove to 20th Century-Fox, where we found Darryl Zanuck striding up and down the biggest office I have ever seen, polo mallet in hand. I did my stuff again and all seemed to be going well until Spyros Skouras joined the meeting. This belligerent Greek was in charge of the studio's chain of movie theaters, and like everyone on that side of the business, knew all the answers. Who needed research? Zanuck, being more intelligent, thought *he* did, and invited Gallup and me to spend the weekend as his guests at the Arrowhead Springs Hotel. What a lark! I started by having a free check-up with the hotel doctor, who gave me a beaker of castor oil, just like Fettes. Then I had a mud bath, and ordered a gargantuan dinner, with a magnum of Lafite. At the next table sat the doctor, eyeing me nervously in case his depth-charge exploded. On Monday morning Schaefer telephoned to say that RKO would give us a twelve-month contract—on an exclusive basis. When Zanuck heard this, he gave orders that Gallup and I were never to be allowed on 20th-Century property again.

We had undertaken to perform four services for RKO:

To measure the popularity of movie stars in terms of their power to sell tickets. I called this the Audit of Marquee Values.

To pretest the audience acceptance of films based on Broadway plays, novels, and original screenplays.

To test the selling power of different *titles* for pictures.

To find out how many moviegoers had heard of each picture before it was released. I called this the Index of Publicity Penetration.

To pretest a story, we showed a synopsis to a cross-section of moviegoers and asked if they would like to see it as a movie. We found that people had a tendency to exaggerate their interest in Abraham Lincoln, but we learned to avoid such traps by first asking respondents if they would prefer to spend the evening listening to a radio comedian like Jack Benny or reading Shakespeare. If they said Shakespeare, we knew they were liars and broke off the interview.

Given a synopsis of the story, the title, and the cast, we were able to predict how many people would see a picture—*before it was made*. Our average error was less than 10 percent. Soon we started recommending our own ideas for pictures and certifying our recommendations with test scores. I recommended David Selznick to make an epic about the life of Jesus Christ, but he funked it. I suggested to Disney that he make *Alice in Wonderland*, and he did so. Sometimes our clients invested big money in buying a story without first running it through our test. It was a ticklish business when I had to tell them that the public had no interest in their purchase. This happened with Paul Gallico's *Snow Goose* and many other admirable properties.

The studio people wasted endless time arguing about titles; we were able to tell them which title would sell the most tickets. When we tested the title *Syncopation*, 43 percent did not even know what the word meant. "Is it some kind of religion?" When we measured "publicity penetration" we found that three moviegoers out of four had not heard of the average picture at the time of its release. The publicity was too little and too late, so the picture could not realize its full potential.

Only a quarter of the population went to the movies in any given week. At first I assumed that the others were too busy listening to the radio, reading, playing cards, or seeing their friends, but this proved to be wrong; we found that they

77

weren't doing *anything*, while the people who often went to the movies also read a lot, *and* listened to the radio *and* led active social lives. As for me, I had to go to the movies three or four times a week, to keep abreast of the product. I have never gone since.

By measuring the popularity of movie stars in terms of their power to sell tickets, I calculated how much each star contributed to the receipts of a picture, and told our clients how much he should be paid. Clark Gable, Spencer Tracy, Mickey Rooney, and Gary Cooper were worth four times as much as Ronald Reagan, Greta Garbo, or Marlene Dietrich.

Every two months I issued charts showing the rise and decline of each star's popularity. It had always been assumed that people went to the movies to ogle the opposite sex. I demonstrated that the exact opposite was the case. When men went to the movies they identified themselves with the *male* star in the picture; among men, the thirteen most popular stars were *men* stars. When women went to the movies they identified with the *female* star. Only Hedy Lamarr and a few other sex symbols were more popular with men than with women. Boys wanted to see boy stars, old women wanted to see old women stars, sophisticated people wanted to see Katharine Hepburn and Laurence Olivier. Uneducated moviegoers plumped for their own kind—Abbott and Costello, Betty Grable, George Raft, etc. I invented a party game. After getting each player to make a list of his six favorite stars, I could identify the author of each list in terms of his age, sex, income, and geographical origin. People voted for the stars who most resembled themselves.

The big stars were convinced that the public would get sick of them if they appeared in more than one picture a year. I demonstrated that this was a fallacy; stars who appeared in only one picture showed an average loss of 17 percent in popularity, while stars who made three pictures a year showed an average gain of nine percent. I discovered that some stars had a *negative* effect at the box office; their names on the marquee repelled more ticket buyers than they attracted. The list, which I called Box Office Poison, and classified TOP SECRET, included some of the most famous names in show business, and ruined their careers. Their personalities dazzled the producers but left the public cold.

In those days the motion picture industry revolved around the stars, and their agents wielded great influence on the studios. Most powerful of all was Dr. Jules Stein, who had been an ophthalmologist. Quick to realize that our surveys were revealing information which was new, he invited me to lunch and picked my brains. When I told him how high his client Lana Turner had risen in our Audit of Marquee Values, he excused himself and went off to negotiate a new contract for her. I had to pay for the lunch.

My father used to say that it was a mistake to meet your favorite author. He had once dined with Sir James Barrie and found out what an odious little creep he was. I found that it was equally a mistake to meet my favorite movie star. One day I had tea with Charles Laughton in his fuchsia garden and found him to be a repulsive egotist. Almost every star I met suffered from this disease. No doubt they had been pleasant enough when they were sodajerks in Des Moines or cowboys in Wyoming, but money and adulation went to their heads. I encountered only two exceptions: Loretta Young, whose Catholic piety kept her humble, and Harpo Marx. Harpo spoke little but laughed loud and often. On a table in his living room I saw a photograph of Roosevelt inscribed, *From your friend*. His harp teacher lived in New York and gave him lessons over long distance telephone. One day Harpo gave a recital. At the end, the audience cheered their heads off, but for several minutes Harpo did not take a bow. He had run around to the back of the auditorium and was leading the applause.

In Los Angeles I met people who were more interesting than the movie stars. Sam Behrman, who was writing *The Cowboy and the Lady* for Gary Cooper. Alfred Hitchcock, who had been an art director in a London advertising agency. Thornton Wilder, who behaved to Aldous Huxley as if he were an ambitious curate and Huxley a bishop. And Sam Goldwyn, who persuaded me to give him the results of a confidential survey and promptly leaked them to the press; I disliked Mr. Goldwyn.

As time went by, high muck-a-mucks in other studios—Louis B. Mayer, David Selznick, Walt Disney, Harry Warner, Walter Wanger, Jack Cohn, and Frank Y. Freeman—showed interest. In due course some of them became our clients. My favorite was David Selznick, who took to ordering surveys the way other people order groceries. During a story conference with Aldous Huxley and Robert Stevenson he telephoned and asked me for a survey to settle an argument they were having about the story line for *Jane Eyre*. "Forget it," I said. "Our tests show that *Jane Eyre* is going to be a flop *whatever* you do. In any case, you should not use research as a substitute for creative judgment."

Selznick's father-in-law, Louis B. Mayer of Metro-Goldwyn-Mayer, had more stars under contract than all the other studios combined. He asked whether I would spend a year at MGM teaching them how to use our research, but this would have meant leaving our other clients in the lurch, so I had to refuse. Mayer was not a creative genius like Selznick, but he had an unrivaled instinct for popular taste.

I could not have had a better boss than Dr. Gallup. His confidence in me was such that I do not recall his ever reading any of the reports I wrote in his name. Once he had worked out the methodology of the research, he lost interest and moved on to something new. However, he took the wise precaution of installing Barbara Benson, his sister-in-law, to keep a professional eye on my shaky research procedures. Gallup had one curious quirk: he paid niggardly wages. I got $40 a week, which was less than the gardeners of the Hollywood moguls I was advising. Saul Rae, who later became Canadian ambassador to the United Nations, was employed to help Gallup write a book —for $50 a week. Jack Tibby, who later became managing editor of *Sports Illustrated*, and Bill Lydgate, who was to become chairman of the Foreign Policy Association, were each paid $100 a week to write the Gallup Poll releases to newspapers. Alfred Max, who was to found a group of French magazines, got $45 a week. I don't think any of us resented this niggardliness—we were learning too much. Indeed, I would have been happy to pay Gallup for the education he gave me. Apart from polling, he taught me three things of consummate value:

1. "Grant graciously what you dare not refuse."

2. "When you don't know the answer, confuse the issue."

3. "When you foul the air in somebody else's bathroom, burn a match and the smell will vanish."

Gallup is a man of remarkable humility. When a magazine published an article attacking his methods on thirty-eight counts, he summoned his lieutenants and told us that he agreed with thirty-six of them.

Anyone who works for a polling organization is constantly subjected to heckling—"I have never been interviewed, and I don't know anybody who has." One evening in Pennsylvania Station an interviewer accosted me, clipboard at the ready. Would I answer a few questions? I had written those questions myself. They sounded so dumb that I went back to my office and canceled the survey.

The job called for me to commute between Princeton and Hollywood. In those days there were no transcontinental airplanes, so I got to see the country from train windows—glamorous trains like the Santa Fe Super Chief and the City of Los Angeles. On one of these journeys I stopped off in San Francisco and spent two days with Albert Bender, an elderly Dubliner who represented Lloyds of London in San Francisco and divided his wealth between young California painters and the Irish Republican Army. On another trip to Hollywood I got off the train in Montana and spent three unforgettable weeks with Harry Hart, an English rancher who had known Bill Hickok and Calamity Jane. He sent me on a pack trip high in the Crazy Mountains. My guide, a young cowboy of Norwegian extraction, told me stories about Jowett and other Oxford figures of the last century; he had heard them from an old Irishman who had once been a don at Balliol and found his way to Montana during a sabbatical, never to leave. When I had to leave those lovely mountains, with their intoxicating atmosphere, their carpets of forget-me-nots and their egalitarian inhabitants, I cried.

In spite of the fact that Gallup paid me only $40 a week, my wife and I contrived to support four refugee children from England, and to live at Mansgrove, the most beautiful eighteenth-century house in Princeton. Our neighbor Jerry Lambert kept us supplied with flowers from his great garden and took us sailing in his yacht *Atlantic*. This three-masted schooner had a crew of thirty-nine and had sailed across the Atlantic Ocean from Sandy Hook to the Lizard in twelve days, four hours, and one minute—the all-time record, not excluding the clippers. Jerry, who had made a quick fortune out of advertising Listerine as a cure for halitosis, maintained a private polling organization and placed it at the disposal of Tom Dewey, who was trying to get the Republican nomination. When Dewey was to make a major speech on foreign policy, Jerry's pollsters prepared short statements which summarized every possible opinion on each major issue. They then showed these statements to a cross-section of voters and asked which most nearly reflected their views. The statement which received the most votes went into the speech. This cynical approach would have won the nomination for Dewey if he had not looked, in Alice Longworth's phrase, like "a little man on a wedding cake." Instead, Wendell Willkie was nominated and Jerry Lambert offered him the same service during the runup to the election; but Willkie was too cocksure to pay attention to public opinion and was duly obliterated by Roosevelt.

Jerry was that rare phenomenon—a successful businessman with a first-class mind. He did double-crostics in his head, without writing them down. When he died, I was one of the pallbearers at his funeral, along with George Gallup, Allen Dulles, Paul Mellon, Hadley Cantril, and Mike Vanderbilt, and I inherited his clothes. They don't fit, but I still wear them—in loving memory.

Our other great friends in Princeton were Beatrice and Bruce Gould, who edited the *Ladies' Home Journal* for twenty-five years. I have always thought that it would be murder to work in the same office as one's wife, but the Goulds thrived on it, as did my friends Henry and Margaret Rudkin at Pepperidge Farm. Last time I saw the Goulds they were swimming in a reservoir; for one hour they never stopped talking to each other. A rare marriage.

My son David Fairfield Ogilvy was born in Princeton. On his first outing, Einstein bent over his pram and infused him with wisdom which has never deserted him. When he was three, our friend and neighbor Edward Howrey described him as "the most perfect human being I have ever known." If I had not preached so loud and so often on the evils of nepotism and inherited management, he would have made the best of all chairmen at Ogilvy & Mather. Instead, he has become a champion Realtor, and my infallible advisor on matters great and small.

Meanwhile, the war was raging in Europe. France had fallen, and the only hope of defeating Hitler lay in American intervention. I had been moonlighting as advisor to the British government on American public opinion, but it was time I played a more active part. The opportunity came in the form of an invitation to join the staff of Sir William Stephenson in the Secret Service.

[4]

Secret Service

T H E war memoirs of British statesmen, generals, and diplomats never refer to the exploits of the Intelligence Service. There are two reasons for this. First, they don't want to run afoul of the Official Secret Act. Second, they share Henry Stimson's prissy view that "gentlemen don't read each other's mail"—and don't want you to know that they were the beneficiaries of such skulduggery.

In recent years the British government has come to realize that this conspiracy of silence has not only falsified history, but has also damaged the reputation of its Secret Service. So the truth is

87

now being allowed to dribble out, aided by the new thirty-year rule. Hence the publication of Sir John Masterman's report on the Double-Cross System, which caught every spy the Germans sent to Britain and converted them into conduits for misleading Hitler. Hence, also, the publication of Fred Winterbotham's book *The Ultra Secret* about the the British achievement in deciphering the radio signals of the German high command.

Sir William Stephenson was, I believe, one of the most effective operators in the long history of the British Secret Service, in a class with Walsingham, Major John André, Mansfield Cumming, Blinker Hall, Sir William Wiseman, and Alastair Denniston. David Bruce has this to say about him:

> It is interesting to reflect on what might have been the fate of Britain, and subsequently the United States, if Sir William Stephenson and his associates, clothed in clandestinity, had not provided an essential complement to military and political measures through covert means. It is difficult for laymen to comprehend how one shadowy figure, through undercover operations, could have exercised on the fate of the Western world an influence so indispensable to its survival.

During the 1914–18 war, Bill Stephenson had won the Distinguished Flying Cross as a fighter pilot, and spent the next twenty years in industry. In 1940 Churchill sent him to the United States as head of all secret missions in the Western Hemisphere. Stephenson established a close relationship with President Roosevelt, who was never comfortable with Ambassadors Lothian and Halifax. (In 1915 President Wilson had established the same kind of relationship with Sir William Wiseman, a young army captain whom Lloyd George had sent to the United States as head of the intelligence mission.)

It suited Roosevelt to use Stephenson as the channel for some of his secret dealings with Churchill before the United States entered the war. Robert Sherwood later told Stephenson, "If the isolationists had known the full extent of the secret alliance between the U.S. and Britain, their demands for the President's impeachment would have rumbled like thunder across the land." Perhaps the most valuable of Stephenson's achievements was to persuade Roosevelt to set up the Office of Strategic Services, and then to help General Donovan organize that formidable organization. Says David Bruce, "With unstinted and constant generosity, Stephenson lent his most trusted subordinates to assist." I was one of those subordinates. After the war, Truman gave Stephenson the Medal of Merit—the first non-American to receive this highest civilian award.

He was a man of extraordinary fertility. All was grist to his mill. It took eleven secretaries to keep up with him. Bernard Baruch said that "Stephenson could think seven stages ahead of you. It was terrifying to watch. When he spoke he cut clean through the matter. Never wasted a word." He was equally laconic in his replies to memoranda —either YES or NO or SPEAK. A few days before Pearl Harbor, he telegraphed to London that a Japanese attack was expected. No such report had come from the Embassy, so Stephenson was asked to identify his source. His reply, laconic as usual: "The President of the United States."

He always listened with total concentration to what I had to say, a sympathetic grin flickering at the corner of his mouth. He never betrayed a personal confidence. I stood in awe of his sagacity. My first assignment was to attend a course for spies and saboteurs at a camp near Toronto. Here I was taught the tricks of the trade. How do you follow people without arousing their suspicion? Walk in *front* of them; if you also push a pram, this will disarm their suspicion still further. I was taught to use a revolver, to blow up bridges and power lines with plastic, to cripple police dogs by grabbing their front legs and tearing their chests apart, and to kill a man with my bare hands. I expected to be parachuted into occupied territory where I could practice these skills, but Stephenson put me in charge of collecting economic intelligence from Latin America, where he had a network of agents. Our primary function was to ruin businessmen whom we knew to be working against the Allies, and to prevent Hitler laying his hands on strategic materials—industrial diamonds, tungsten, vanadium, antimony, etc. I came to know more about these matters than anyone in Washington, and was able to give OSS an average of forty reports a day.

It was difficult to avoid getting impaled on the rivalries which bristled between OSS, the FBI, and other branches of the American intelligence community. Some of my colleagues regarded the FBI as flatfoots, but the FBI's penetration of Russian clandestine activities was exemplary. Thousands of American and British sailors were being drowned delivering the supplies which saved the Russians from defeat, but this did not deter Stalin from unrelenting espionage against our governments. Donald Maclean was Stalin's spy at the British embassy. Kim Philby was his spy at SIS headquarters in London. And the defection of Igor Gouzenko from the Russian embassy in Ottawa—Bill Stephenson's last case—revealed that the Canadian, British, and United States governments were honeycombed with Russian agents, some at high levels.

When the importance of Latin America

dwindled, I took on other chores, most of them
rather small beer. Stephenson used me to investi-
gate leaks, as when Drew Pearson printed a Top
Secret telegram from Churchill to the British general commanding in Greece; the leaker in this case
was Sumner Welles, the Undersecretary of State.
I was to learn that American newspapers put freedom of the press above the national interest, as
when Colonel McCormick revealed in the Chicago
Tribune that the U.S. Navy had cracked the Japanese naval cipher. This act of treachery could have
lost the war in the Pacific—if the Japanese had
read the *Tribune*.

In his biography of Stephenson,* Montgomery
Hyde says that I was "perhaps the most remarkable of the younger men to join Stephenson." In
my judgment, John Pepper, Louis Frank, and
Gilbert Highet were far more effective, not least
because Stephenson failed to exploit my knowledge
of public opinion. I wrote a paper on the subject
which deserved to be taken more seriously than
it was. Hyde tells the story:

> His knowledge of Gallup's methods led
> David Ogilvy to the conclusion that polls, if
> secretly organized in other countries, could
> assist in settling many political and ethnologi-
> cal problems. These ideas were set out in a re-
> port, entitled *A Plan for Predetermining the*

* *The Quiet Canadian.*

Results of Plebiscites, Predicting the Reactions of People to the Impact of Projected Events, and Applying the Gallup Technique to Other Fields of Secret Intelligence, which was written by Ogilvy and forwarded by Stephenson to London in August, 1943. Although it was received without enthusiasm at the time, both by the British Embassy in Washington and S.I.S. Headquarters in London, the fact remains that a year later the Psychological Warfare Board of General Eisenhower's Headquarters staff successfully carried out polls in Europe in the manner advocated by Ogilvy.

I also functioned as a Second Secretary on the staff of the Embassy. Here the game was to see how many telegrams I could get approved by the hypercritical levels above me; my record was forty-two in four weeks. They were addressed to the Foreign Secretary or the Prime Minister, and signed by Ambassador Halifax. I marvel at my ability to write with the austerity that was required, and to master the complexity of the subjects. Consider, for example, this passage from a telegram I sent to the War Cabinet Office in August 1944:

We have told the State Department of our fear that when Russian military requirements taper off at the end of the German war, which may not be far off, we may be confronted with massive demands for food, textiles and other relief requirements—demands which, if they were granted the supply priority accorded to Protocol requirements, might well absorb relief supplies earmarked for other areas. State Department points out that this has not yet come to pass, and that the wording of the Fourth Protocol does not commit them to automatic acceptance of any revisions proposed by the Russians. However, they recognize that if they treat *all* Russian supplies as coming within the Protocol procedure as regards priority, while we treat part of the Russian requests as being of a lower degree of urgency, the difference may cause substantial confusion in handling.

And so on for 1,700 words, all of which had to be enciphered—by hand, in those days—and then deciphered in London. Brevity was discouraged; it might cause misunderstanding.

Here is the beginning of a sententious telegram I sent to London and Chungking in June 1945:

China is now in the eighth year of her war against Japanese aggression, a war which has brought misery and destitution to a large part of the Chinese people. Over three million Chinese have been killed in battle, and fifty million civilians are reported to be homeless.

It is to the interest of His Majesty's Government that the great Republic of China,
containing a fourth of the population of the
globe, should be set on the road to recovery
as early as possible.

Late on the night I telegraphed these worthy sen-
timents, the cipher office at the Embassy called me
at home. "There's been a mistake. Your telegram
has been sent to Chungking *en clair!*" When the
Chinese authorities intercepted and read it, they
must have thought that we had sent it *en clair*
on purpose, to suck up. Such Sinophile views were
rarely expressed by British officials.

Sometimes I had to secure the agreement of
other Embassies before communicating British
views to the State Department. The Dutch, Belgians, French, Australians, New Zealanders, Ca-
nadians and South Africans were invariably co-
operative, but the Indians were not. It was not their
Ambassador, the enchanting Sir Girja Shankar
Bajpai, who gave me trouble, but his deputy, an
Englishman in the Indian civil service. His loyalty
to India was such that he got me into hot water
by complaining to Lord Halifax that I had no right
to *assume* that the government of India would
support the British Government.

The French were always helpful, provided I did
not have to deal with more than one of them at a
time. When I was instructed by London to help

them procure American locomotives for the French railways, I had to listen for several hours while a group of French experts argued with each other about which type of locomotive would suit them best. My report:

> We have spoken to the French. They remind us that after the last war they were obliged to inherit 2,000 inefficient locomotives from the American military and do not want to repeat the experience. They are, however, impressed with the news that the Inter-Allied experts in London have approved the Mikado design submitted by a representative of the Association of American Locomotive Manufacturers. We seem to have aroused the French here to the urgency of the situation.

My favorite among the ambassadors was **Sir Owen Dixon** of Australia. He regaled me with indiscreet stories about the abominable behavior of Herbert Evatt, who, as the Australian foreign minister, was his chief. Felix Frankfurter considered Dixon the greatest lawyer and judge in the English-speaking world; he ended his career as Chief Justice of Australia.

The British government and the United States government had a habit of sending identical instructions to their Ambassadors in Moscow, and I belonged to an Anglo-American committee which drafted some of them. We seldom had any difficulty agreeing *what* to say, but it was often embarrassing to tell State Department officials—most of them Wall Street lawyers—that their drafting was so ham-fisted that neither Ambassador would be able to understand them. However, I had no difficulty understanding this momentous communication from Cordell Hull to Lord Halifax:

> The Secretary of State presents his compliments to His Excellency the British Ambassador and takes pleasure in informing him that the appropriate Customs Officer has been authorized to admit *free of duty* three cases of whisky for the personal use of Mr. David Ogilvy.

My diplomatic whisky cost $1 a bottle, and I was allowed to import cigars in the diplomatic bag from Havana—15 cents for a long Monte Cristo. When a busybody in the Foreign Office withdrew these traditional privileges from the diplomats in the American Embassy in London, it took the State Department only half an hour to retaliate in kind against the British Embassy in Washington, and another half an hour to negotiate a return to the status quo. I have never seen diplomacy work so fast.

The only thing we lacked was *leadership*. Ambassador Halifax was extremely religious. When he was Viceroy of India, the Governor of Burma had said of him, "when Edward is perplexed he takes his troubles to the Lord, and I regret to say that he often comes away exceedingly ill-advised." He was a curiously lazy man. Every afternoon I saw him set off on a long walk with his wife and their dachshund. He presided over meetings of the heads of various British missions—Embassy, Food, Raw Materials, Treasury, Shipping, Supply —but restricted their frequency to once a fortnight and recorded in his diary, "I don't let it last more than an hour and a quarter." At the Embassy he could not be bothered to see anybody below the rank of Minister, and even those exalted personages complained of his aloofness. The rest of his staff seldom set eyes on him. All his speeches were ghost-written, and he invariably blue-penciled the most interesting passages, afterward complaining that they were not given sufficient prominence in the newspapers.

Incoming telegrams went first to the most junior diplomat concerned with the subject. He wrote his "minute" and passed it up to his boss, and so on until the telegram reached the Ambassador, who sometimes sent them to an even higher authority, with this minute: "Lady H, what do you think?"

When he invited my opposite number in the United States Government to lunch at the Embassy, it did not occur to him to include me. But he was sore as hell when Churchill failed to include him in his meetings with Roosevelt. He seldom bothered to report what he heard from the stream of important Americans who called on him. I volunteered to save him trouble by installing a microphone, so that important conversations could be recorded and summarized by his staff. Needless to say, this was considered ungentlemanly. In those days it was the fashion for diplomats to regard intelligence officers as unprincipled ruffians. We returned the compliment by regarding the diplomats as ceremonial and gutless. With a foot in both camps, I was able to judge the validity of both stereotypes. Yes, many intelligence officers *were* unprincipled; they were occasionally known to commit blackmail, corruption, robbery, and even murder. But, with rare exceptions, they were patriotic men and women, and much of what they achieved was of value. By the same token, some of the diplomats *were* gutless, but they were superbly educated, and were able to cope with subjects whose complexity would have defeated the average intelligence officer.

> *As my old father used to say*
> *When the vicar came to call,*
> *He's not my sort, but pass the port,*
> *Thank God there's room for all.*

Among the British diplomats I particularly cherished Sir George Sansom, a distinguished au-

99

thority on Japan. Lunching one day in the Embassy cafeteria, he looked at me quizzically over his glasses. "That was a very naughty telegram you sent to the Cabinet Office yesterday. Great careers in the Diplomatic Service have been based on just such trivia. As a young Third Secretary in Tokyo, it fell to me to accompany Bernard Shaw when he was received by the Mikado. My report on the interview was entirely frivolous, but it was widely circulated in London and was the foundation of my career."

The diplomatic staff of the Embassy numbered only fifty. Five were Fellows of All Souls and three were future heads of the Diplomatic Service. Eighteen have subsequently been given peerages or knighthoods. In this company I was out of my depth. I did not even *look* like a diplomat. An elderly black lady mistook me for a porter in Union Station and tipped me when I carried her luggage. When I asked a taxi driver to take me to the Embassy, he was clearly surprised.

"You *work* there?" he asked.

"Yes."

"What are you, a gardener?"

"No."

"You speak English pretty good."

"Thank you."

"Did you learn it before you came over?"

"Yes."

My best friend on the staff of the Embassy was

Hadley, who collected the "confidential waste" for incineration. A Highlander and thus no respecter of persons, he had been the chauffeur to a long line of Ambassadors, including Lord Bryce, who wrote the famous book on the American Constitution. When Lord Grey, the ornithologist Foreign Secretary, went to Washington in 1919, he was almost blind and used to take Hadley on birding expeditions in Rock Creek Park. "Hadley, I think I hear a Prairie Warbler. Can you see it? What does it look like?" One day Hadley was driving Grey and a party of British cabinet ministers through the Zoo. Suddenly the bearded face of the headkeeper appeared at the window of the car. "Mr. Lord Ambassador, the rats are raising hell in my duck house. What shall I do?" "Pour boiling oil down their holes," said Grey, and the car drove on. Hadley's pet aversion was Sir Ronald Lindsay, who had been Ambassador in the thirties. "Lindsay was a terrible snob, but he always sat in front beside me, and I used to talk to him man to man. One day he complained that I was too frank. Well, I said, if you think that, you should sit in the back. If you sit beside me, you are Ronald Lindsay." Hadley had made generations of British diplomats rich by advising them to buy real estate in Georgetown when it was still a slum.

About this time my cousin Basil Bleck came to Washington and told me of an incident which had taken place at the end of the Churchill-Roosevelt conference in Casablanca. On the last morning, after the official business was finished, Churchill sent for his security officer. He had just finished breakfast at the Villa Mirador and was lying in bed smoking a cigar. When the security officer entered the bedroom, Churchill looked up at him and said, "I want to visit the bazaars." The security officer said that he would have to consult his American colleagues. The Americans vetoed the expedition as too dangerous. The security officer knew that Churchill did not like being thwarted, but he was an ingenious fellow. He said to the Prime Minister, "Sir, the Americans don't want you to go. They have a report that German assassins have been parachuted around Casablanca, and there is no time to clear the streets where the bazaars are situated. I have explained to them that you are indifferent to all considerations of personal safety, but I must point out that the bazaars are full of disease. If you were to catch one of these diseases, it wouldn't matter—you have the constitution of an ox. But I must remind you that President Roosevelt is an invalid. If he caught the disease from you, the consequences might be tragic."

"All right," Churchill replied, "I won't go. However, I would like you to know that I was not planning to visit the bazaars for the purpose you seem to have in mind. And even if I had been, and had I had the misfortune to contract one of those diseases to which you are evidently referring, I can assure you that I would not have transmitted it to the President of the United States."

All Stephenson's geese were swans. When the war came to an end and his labyrinthine apparatus was dismantled, he praised my "keen analytical powers and special aptitude for handling problems of extreme delicacy . . . not only a good intelligence officer, but a brilliant one." If I give myself Alpha for the work I was later to do on Madison Avenue, I cannot claim more than Beta-minus for my performance in Washington.

It occurred to me that the network of British, American, and Canadian businessmen who had been my colleagues in economic warfare could be converted into a profitable company of merchant adventurers. I wrote a prospectus which appealed to Stephenson, and the company was duly floated, with Ed Stettinius and many top sawyers from the intelligence community as shareholders, including General Donovan, David Bruce, and Sir Charles Hambro. John Pepper was president, and for a few weeks I was vice-president, but the work bored me and I resigned; after that the company never looked back.

How can God-fearing democracies maintain effective intelligence services without compromising civil rights? The answer does not lie in making those services subordinate to leaky committees of self-serving politicians, but in appointing men of integrity to run them, men who can be relied upon not to abuse their power. Gilbert's Pirate King said it all in *The Pirates of Penzance:*

> *But many a King on first-class throne*
> *If he wants to call his crown his own*
> *Must manage somehow to get through*
> *More dirty work than ever I do.*

$$\begin{bmatrix} 5 \end{bmatrix}$$

A Very Large
Rural Monastery

O N a fine evening in June 1940, George Gallup
and I were going to Chicago when we saw from
the train window a group of men who looked
like Pilgrim Fathers. Gallup said they were Amish.
Three weeks later my wife and I took our bicycles
to Lancaster, Pennsylvania, and set out in search
of them. After riding for two days, we found ourselves on the outskirts of Intercourse, and there
on the porch of a spick-and-span farmhouse, we
saw a stack of wide-awake hats. It was Sunday
morning and the Amish were having church.

They had emigrated from South Germany in
the middle of the eighteenth century in search of

religious freedom, and found it in Pennsylvania, where they have lived for two hundred years, isolated from their neighbors and aloof from change. Every detail of their lives is governed by the rigid traditions of their church. They are not allowed cars, but drive buggies. They farm with horses instead of tractors. They are not allowed electricity, but light their houses with candles and oil lamps. No radios, no television, no cinema, no telephones.

The local postmaster found us an Amish family who would take lodgers, and there my wife and I spent every weekend I could escape from Washington: three nights and sixteen meals for $15. Lancaster County had been settled by Englishmen, and the villages still bear English names—Intercourse, Bird in Hand, Paradise, Fertility, Blue Ball, White Horse, Honey Brook. (Intercourse had originally been called Cross Keys, but in the 1840s the burghers decided that it was unseemly for their town to carry the name of an inn, and changed it to Intercourse.)

Sara Fisher, our Amish landlady, bore an extraordinary resemblance to Queen Victoria in old age, but was blessed with a Rabelaisian sense of humor and was a superlative cook. She introduced us to Joas Yoder, a retired Amish farmer of seventy-nine who had seven children under twelve. This dear man spent several afternoons driving us around the country lanes in his carriage, explaining Amish ways. The smells of honeysuckle in the hedges and clover in the fields are with me to this day. The atmosphere was one of serenity, abundance, and contentment. As Lord Snowdon has said, visiting the Amish is like visiting a very large rural monastery.

Joas introduced us to his niece Annie and her husband Levi Fisher, and they invited us to visit them. The first night a hurricane blew the roof off their house, an adventure which led to their becoming our dearest friends. Years later, when they came to visit us in Connecticut, Annie told us that it was the first morning since she was twelve that she had not milked a cow before breakfast.

Most Amishmen are farmers, and those who are not farmers are carpenters, harness makers, carriage builders, blacksmiths, or furniture makers. They work fifteen hours a day. Their wives sit down only to make clothes for their husbands and their children. The women part their hair in the middle, braid it into a bun and cover it with a cap of demure white organdy. Their dresses are made of cotton in solid colors, reaching to the ground. They wear a white dress only once in their lives, on their wedding day. It is then put away in a chest until they die, when they are buried in it.

The men wear long hair and beards, but no mustaches, because their tradition has it that mustaches are military, and they are pacifists. Their

107

suits are black. Their jackets have no collars, lapels or outside pockets, and are fastened with hooks and eyes, buttons also being regarded as military. Their trousers are of the barn-door variety, opening at the sides instead of in front. In winter they wear heavy black capes and hats of black felt; the church decrees that the flat crowns have to be three and a half inches high and the brims four inches wide. Their summer hats are the same shape but are made of straw from their own wheat. The children wear miniature replicas of their parents' dress and look like dolls.

At first sight the Amish give an impression of rather forbidding austerity, but I have never known people so addicted to high-jinks. At our first Amish luncheon party, the conversation turned to the fact that my wife and I had only one child. This struck them as bizarre and a venerable great-grandmother suggested that my wife should "get a new rooster." Their own families are enormous—an average of eight children, and sixteen is by no means unheard of. An Amishman who died in 1930 left five hundred and sixty-five direct descendants, and another left four hundred and ten. Malinda Stoltzfus left three hundred and forty-three, and Barbara Fisher left three hundred and twenty-four. The result of this fertility is that the Amish population has increased five-fold since the turn of the century.

108

You might suppose that inbreeding in this genetically isolated community would produce unfortunate consequences. I know of only one, a form of dwarfism which is unique to the Amish. Their dwarfs have six fingers and malformed hearts and are all descended from Samuel King, an eighteenth-century Amishman who was not himself a dwarf. However, up to 1964 there had been only twenty-four cases in two hundred years. Apart from this, the Amish are singularly robust, intelligent, and long-lived.

One Amish family in every four is called Stoltzfus (Proudfoot), and seven surnames account for 77 percent of all families: Stoltzfus, King, Beiler, Fisher, Lapp, Zook, and Esh. The boys are given Old Testament names like Moses, Jacob, Samuel, Abraham, Isaac, David, Jonathan, Daniel, Amos, Tobias, Benjamin—and Christ (pronounced to rhyme with *list*). The girls are called Mary, Annie, Katie, Sarah, Fannie, Barbara, Rebecca, Lizzie, Sadie, Malinda.* With such a limited roster of names, you find four or five Isaac Fishers, Jacob Kings, and Daniel Beilers living within a few miles of each other. Confusion is avoided by the fact that most of them have nicknames. I knew a white-bearded deacon who was universally known as Shitting Abe; he

* They give their horses English names like Jim, Harry, Charlie, Tom, and Frank.

had been incontinent as a little boy. Another patriarch was known as Pepper Dan; seventy years before he had made his teacher sneeze by putting pepper on the school stove. Another was Double Decker Ben; you could drive a wagon into his barn on two decks instead of the usual one. Then there were Baldy Dave, Crusher John, Squirrely Joe, and Black Jake, who made the best toys I have ever seen.*

They talk a German dialect among themselves, but learn to speak English when they go to school, a curious mixture of archaic English and direct translations from their German. One day when I was driving an Amish family in my car, one of the children farted. "What for foul air, Amos?" asked his mother. You hear them say that a farm was "drecky" until an Amishman bought it, and now it is "all red-up." At the end of a party, when the ice cream (a quart a head) is finished, they say, "the ice cream is all." An Amish woman told me that her bedridden father-in-law had "beshitted" himself the night before.

"Run the stairs up and shut the window down."

"It wonders me what he paid for that horse."

"Is your grandmother living yet?"

"Spritz the tobacco bed."

"Outen the light."

---

*Somewhat similar nicknames are used in the pueblos of Andalusia.

"Alright already."

"Davy is wonderful sick."

"We live neighbors to them."

They use *dare* in its archaic form *durst*—"you *durst* have some more apple butter." And the plural of *you* is *youns*—"*youns* are welcome."

And welcome we were. It has always been a mystery to me why so many Amish were so kind to us. Perhaps it was that we did not try to photograph them; they take literally the commandment that "thou shalt not make to thyself any graven image, nor the *likeness* of anything." We kept the sabbath, and were never seen to drink alcohol. And we were not in any way like their Mennonite neighbors, whom they dislike as much as the Dutch dislike the Belgians.

In 1946 I left London and flew to Baltimore, seventeen turbulent hours in a flying boat. My wife met me and we drove to Bishop Lapp's farm near Intercourse. The house had been built in 1856, of Georgian brick with white shutters. The upstairs was all one room and had been a miniature ballroom in pre-Amish days. It was for sale and the Bishop knew I had set my heart on buying it. "David," he said, "I cannot sell it to you. My people think you might start a beer parlor or build an airport." It was no use pleading that the two things I hate most in the world are airports and bars. However, a few months later another farm

111

came up for sale, and by getting an Amish friend to bid for me, I succeeded in buying it. A hundred acres of limestone land, a huge bank barn, and two houses for $23,500. A trout stream flowed through the meadow. There were kingfishers, mallard, and killdeers, and great drifts of *Scilla siberica*. Here we settled down to live, my wife and I with our four-year-old son, surrounded by Amish.

Within their community they lead an extremely active social life. Every other Sunday there is church, which brings people together like a meet of foxhounds. On alternate Sundays they drive off on a round of visits, or stay at home and receive. This perpetual entertaining requires Amish housewives to keep their larders lavishly stocked; some of them bottle five hundred quarts of fruit, vegetables, and beef stew every year. The convention is that when guests come to luncheon, every inch of the table must be covered with dishes of meat, gravy, salad, potatoes, pickles, pies, jam, and cake. They have gargantuan appetites but work so hard that they never get fat. However, I am sorry to say that most of them have complete sets of false teeth before they are thirty. I don't know the reason for this, unless it is that the children never drink milk.

Their confidence in doctors is limited, and they are suckers for every kind of quack. "Electric water" is their treatment of choice for a wide variety of diseases, and they rely heavily on pow-wow doctors, whose treatment consists of incantations. When Joseph Yoder was fifteen, he ran a dung fork into his foot and a few hours later was in agony. His mother stroked her hand across the wound three times, and in two minutes the pain had gone.

One of the most enviable things about the Amish is the respect in which they hold their elders. I have never heard an Amish child be impertinent to his parents. When a father gets too old to farm, he turns over the land to his youngest son and moves into the dower house—*das grossdadei heisli*. But his son continues to take his advice, and his wife does duty as a built-in baby-sitter. There are no such things as old folks homes.

The Amish think it is pointless for their children, who are destined to spend their lives farming, to learn more than reading, writing, and arithmetic, and refuse to send them to school after they are fourteen.* This has brought them into constant collision with the laws of Pennsylvania and other states, and I have known Amishmen go to prison over it. I heard one Amish farmer say, "When young people are through high school they don't want to do anything unless they can do it sit-

---

* Here they rely on I Corinthians 3:19: "The wisdom of this world is foolishness with God."

ting down. It spoils them for farming. And when girls are out of college, they want to live out of tin cans. A man might as well marry a can opener."

In 1971 the State of Wisconsin took the issue to the Supreme Court. Because the Amish are not allowed by their church to engage in any form of litigation, they could not defend themselves, but some well-wishers, of whom I was one, engaged William B. Ball of Harrisburg to represent them. The case turned on whether the State's compulsory school attendance law was valid under the Free Exercise clause of the First Amendment of the U.S. Constitution—freedom of religion. Mr. Ball told the Court that *the purpose of Amish education was not to get ahead in the world but to get to heaven.* The Court's decision was unanimous in favor of the Amish, Chief Justice Burger pronouncing that "compulsory school attendance to age sixteen for Amish children carries with it a very real threat of undermining the Amish community and religious practice." (Loud and prolonged cheers.)

Archibald MacLeish has written:

The usual view of the Amish is that they are an anachronism, a people who got stuck in history back with the horse and wagon and an Old Testament God and other chronological oddities, such as the art of husbandry,

114

and domestic skills long unused, and harmonious lives. . . . The Amish have reason to believe that they and their fathers and their fathers' fathers have been wiser about the world than the forebears of the gawking tourists. . . . At a time when we believed in our innocence that the cotton gin and the railroad train and the flying machine and the internal combustion engine knew where they were going . . . the Amish had already decided that they weren't joining the procession.

If you ever become a hobo and walk the roads, I recommend Lancaster County. The Amish will never refuse you a meal, and will allow you to sleep in their barns. Some hoboes, after spending the winter in the workhouse, return to Lancaster summer after summer; like Old Stinky, who made roses out of crinkly paper in return for his food. He stayed so long at our farm that every room was a bower of roses before he moved on. However, sleeping in barns is no longer very comfortable now that farmers stack their hay in bales. A roll in the hay is a thing of the past. You cannot roll in bales.

By the same token, if you are black, have the misfortune to be trapped in an urban slum, and are out of work, move to Lancaster County. I promise that you will find work, and the Amish will shower kindness on you. They know what Christian means.

They are not impressed by riches or rank. One day I took Gladwyn Jebb to call on an elderly Amishman who looked like St. Peter; the man was dozing in a hammock between two flowering apple trees. Without getting up he asked Jebb who he was. "I am the British Ambassador to the United Nations." The old man thought this over for a minute or two. "Quite a big shot, ain't you?"

There is nothing namby-pamby about them. Until they marry and settle down, the boys are pretty wild. They buy trotters off the race track and drive them at breakneck speed. They hold buggy races down the main street of Intercourse on Sunday evenings, accompanied by blood-curdling yells. And their first babies are usually born less than nine months after they get married.

The church is organized in parishes of about forty families, each presided over by a bishop, two preachers, and an almoner. These men are farmers who left school at fourteen, but many of them know the New Testament by heart from beginning to end. Their election is entrusted to God, through the medium of a lottery. They rule their parishioners with a rod of iron. Anyone caught owning a tractor, or committing adultery, or stealing is excommunicated by bell, book, and candle. Not only is the sinner excluded from Communion, he is totally ostracized. Even his own family is forbidden to dine at the same table.* I have heard that his wife may not share his bed. This awful discipline has been a powerful force in preserving the Amish way of life.

There are material advantages to being Amish. If you break your leg, your nearest neighbor does your plowing. If your barn burns down, and many do, your neighbors build you a new one. If you die and leave your family in poverty, the almoner takes care of them.

Their religious services are held on alternate Sundays, not in a church building, but in farmhouses, a relic from the days when they were persecuted in Germany. The houses are built with partitions which can be folded back to form a space big enough for the whole congregation. The day before it is your turn to "have church," a wagon arrives with the benches, trestle tables, and hymn books—the Ausbund, first printed in Switzerland in 1564. At eight o'clock on Sunday morning the congregation drives up in buggies and carriages. The service starts with an introductory sermon, which lasts half an hour and is in Palatine German. This is followed by silent prayers and the lesson of the day. The main sermon, or *gemeh*

---

* "If any man that is called a brother be a fornicator, or covetous, or an idolator, or a railer, or a drunkard, or an extortioner, with such an one *no not to eat*." I Corinthians, 5:11.

halde, is usually preached by the Bishop, and he takes at least an hour; one envies the mothers who are allowed to take their babies out to the summer kitchen and nurse them, a spectacle much appreciated by my four-year-old son.

When the main sermon is finished, the other preachers comment on it, at length. Then come hymns, sung in unison, without accompaniment, devoid of rhythm, at a funereal pace, and with a tremolo which the Amish call *zutterich singe.* These melancholy dirges, which have never been written down, derive from Gregorian chanting and from incongruous German folk songs like "I Saw the Lord of Frankenstein" and "I Saw a Maiden with a Jug." Some of the hymns extend to sixty verses and recount the sufferings of Anabaptist martyrs in the sixteenth century.[*]

Finally, after three hours of preaching and praying and caterwauling, the service ends with the benediction. At the words *Durch Jesum Christum*, the congregation genuflects, which is surprising in such a super-Protestant church.

Then comes lunch, and it is always the same: soup, pickled eggs, beetroot, snitz pie, cheese and coffee. The grownups spend the afternoon lazing on the lawn and the children play games, until it is time for everyone to drive home and milk their cows.

---

[*] My farmer Toby Stoltzfus used to sing them to the cows when he was milking; it increased their yield.

My wife was sometimes invited to quilting bees, which last all day and are more productive than bridge parties. When an Amish family wants to add a room to their house or change the configuration of their stables, they invite their neighbors to a sort of working feast, called a *frolic*. They never pass up an opportunity to attend an auction. When a farm is sold, the auctioneer adjourns the bidding halfway through and gives the bidders half an hour to borrow more capital from their parents, uncles, and grandfathers. Hamburgers and hot dogs are provided, and an enjoyable time is had by all.

Instead of dances, Amish teenagers have "singings" on Sunday nights. The proceedings start with hymns and end with square dances. The boys arrive in open buggies with their sisters, but leave with somebody else's sister.

In winter, when snow covers the roads, they bring out their sleighs and drive them at breakneck speed. Sleighbells are forbidden by the church, so you cannot hear them coming until they are on top of you. More than once I had to throw myself into a snowdrift to avoid being run down.

Next to milk, the most important cash crop is tobacco for cigars. Tobacco requires an exorbitant amount of hand labor, so the more children you have, the more tobacco you can grow. The work starts between February and April, when an antique steam engine comes to sterilize your seed bed. The seed is so fine that, to sow it evenly, you have to suspend it in water and sprinkle it on the seed bed with a watering can. The Amish were vastly amused when a well-meaning Congressman from an urban constituency proposed that no farmer should be allowed more than a *bushel* of tobacco seed, in the belief that this would make more land available for wheat. He was not aware that a bushel will produce enough tobacco plants for *seven thousand* acres. Few Amishmen grow more than *five* acres.

After sowing, you cover the seed bed with bristles from the last hog you butchered, and cover the bristles with muslin. If you keep spritzing the bed, the seedlings will be eight inches high by the end of May. You then transplant them to the field, five thousand plants to an acre, watering each one as you plant it.

As the plants grow, you keep the weeds under control by hoeing. Around the middle of August you break the top off each plant—five thousand plants to an acre—so that its strength will go into the lateral leaves. Two weeks later you go through the field again, removing side shoots and huge green caterpillars; sticky work. By the middle of September, the plants are ready to cut, provided they have not been smashed to ribbons by hail or pock-marked beyond redemption by a fungus disease called wildfire. You cut the plants with shears at ground level—one of the most tiring jobs in the farming calendar. After leaving them to wilt in the sun for a few hours, you spear the plants onto wooden laths, five plants to a lath. Then you hang the laths on a vehicle called a tobacco ladder and drive it to the barn. If your horses get bored waiting, they bolt. The sight of a tobacco ladder careering across the landscape behind a pair of galloping Percherons, loaded with your assets, is pretty terrifying. When the tobacco finally reaches the barn, you hang the laths on scaffolding, which requires dangerous climbing. During the next few weeks you pray for dry weather so that the tobacco will cure instead of rot. In November you take it down from the scaffolding—golden, fragrant, fragile, and thin as tissue paper. Then you remove the leaves from each stalk, sort them by sizes, tie them into hands, bale them in a wooden press, wrap the bales in brown paper, and tie the bales with twine. By keeping at it, I could strip five hundred plants in a ten-hour day. Finally a buyer from one of the cigar companies calls on you and tries to buy your tobacco. My first year, one of these scoundrels offered me 28 cents a pound and swore that mine was the last crop he was authorized to buy at that price. So I sold. The following morning the same buyer paid my neighbor 41 cents a pound. A group of Amish farmers got fed up with such chicanery, and organized a public auction. The buyers came to the sale, *but not a single bid was offered*. A collusive conspiracy if ever I saw one. The experiment had to be abandoned and we farmers found ourselves where we had started, alone in our barns at the mercy of the unscrupulous buyers.

What a pity Willa Cather did not know the Amish. I know only two books on the subject which are worth reading. The first is a monograph by the Reverend Calvin Bachman, published in 1942 by the Pennsylvania German Society. Bachman was the minister of the United Church of Christ near Intercourse for forty-one years, and the only outsider who knew more about the Amish than I did. The second is *Rosanna of the Amish*, by Joseph W. Yoder, an Amishman who defected to go to college. It tells the life story of his mother, an Irish orphan who was adopted by an Amish family. In its primitive way *Rosanna* is as moving as Cather's *My Ántonia*.

A few years ago a group of local entrepreneurs started exploiting the Amish as a tourist attraction. Every Saturday and Sunday in summer, scores of buses now converge on Intercourse from New York and Philadelphia, and decant their loathsome cargoes of trippers, armed with cameras. The contrast between the vulgarity of these urban barbarians and the dignity of the Amish is dramatic. A more serious threat to the Amish comes from within their community. The stiff-necked refusal of their bishops to allow motorcars and tractors has placed an acute strain on the obedience of their parishioners. If you plow your field with horses at three miles an hour while your non-Amish neighbor on the other side of the fence is plowing with a tractor, you cannot be blamed for asking what Biblical authority your bishop has for forbidding tractors. In due course you may join a like-minded group of rebels in starting a new denomination. This had happened some time before I went to Lancaster County. The breakaway group drove not only tractors but also motorcars. They covered the chromium on their cars with black paint and were thus known as "Black Bumper" Amish. Other schisms have been caused by disagreements over such issues as dress and hair style. By 1940 there were six distinct denominations of Amish, covering the spectrum from ultra-conservative to relatively liberal. None of these schisms had anything to do with doctrine; all the Amish denominations have the same articles of faith. I am on the side of the old guard; but I don't have to plow with horses.

Strict as they are in obedience to their own rules, the Amish are remarkably tolerant of people whose churches allow them to lead more worldly lives. "You have your ways, and we have ours." This habit of tolerance allowed them to use our telephone and to cadge rides in our car. "Will you haul me to Bird in Hand? I have to get my cabbage plants." It was a raffish spectacle to see half a dozen Amishmen bowling along in our Model A Ford.

The years we spent in Lancaster County were the richest of my life. But it became apparent that I could never earn my living as a farmer. I *worried* too much. I worried about the price of tobacco and cabbage and wheat. I worried about floods—it can rain pitchforks and sawlogs in Lancaster. I was not physically strong enough to do the work. I found hoeing weeds and topping tobacco unbearably tedious. I was not sufficiently mechanical to keep the farm machinery in repair. I was ignorant of animal husbandry, which cannot be learned out of books. The final humiliation came when Bishop Ira Stoltzfus and his six sons were helping me fill my silo with corn fodder; the Bishop was obliged to ask that I get out of their way.

I remembered how my grandfather had failed as a farmer and become a successful businessman. Why not follow in his footsteps? Why not start an advertising agency? I was thirty-eight.

[6]

Fame and Fortune

I had no credentials, no clients, and only $6,000 in the bank. Today, twenty-eight years later, Ogilvy & Mather has become one of the five biggest advertising agencies in the world, with offices in twenty-nine countries, a thousand clients, and billings of $800,000,000 a year.

If you want to follow my example, here is the recipe: First, make a reputation for being a creative genius. Second, surround yourself with partners who are better than you are. Third, leave them to get on with it.

I wrote my first advertisement when I was thirty-nine. But unlike most beginners, I already

125

knew a lot about advertising. Dr. Gallup had taught me what he had discovered about the factors which make advertisements succeed or fail. Rosser Reeves had taught me what he had learned from disciples of Claude Hopkins. I had picked the brains of John Caples, Jerry Lambert, and other pioneers. And I had read all the books about advertising, such as they were. When I put this knowledge to use, and added a pinch of imagination, I was able to produce a series of campaigns which, almost overnight, made Ogilvy & Mather famous. They included these:

> For Hathaway shirts I used a model with a black patch over his eye. This campaign ran for nineteen years and has recently been revived.

> For Schweppes I persuaded the client, Commander Whitehead, to appear in his own advertisements. This campaign ran for eighteen years.

> For Guinness I created a series of guides— to oysters, cheese, game birds, etc.

> For Rolls-Royce I used the headline, At 60 Miles an Hour the Loudest Noise in This New Rolls-Royce Comes from the Electric Clock. This remains the most famous automobile advertisement of all time.

126

For Puerto Rico I created a campaign which attracted hundreds of factories and millions of tourists.

For Shell I created a campaign which, for the first time in the history of the oil industry, explained the *ingredients* of gasoline.

For Dove I advertised "one quarter cleansing-cream, Dove will cream your skin while you wash." This campaign is still running.

For Sears Roebuck I created advertisements which extolled the policies and services of Sears, instead of their merchandise.

I doubt whether any copywriter has ever produced so many winners in such a short period. The ideas came to me when the telephone line from my unconscious was functioning—when I was at stool, or tipsy, or asleep. They made Ogilvy & Mather so hot that getting clients was like shooting fish in a barrel.

I doubt if any advertising agency has ever had such a distinguished roster of clients. In addition to the United States Government, the British Government, the French Government, and the Government of Puerto Rico, we won American Express, Campbell Soup Company, General Foods, IBM, Merrill Lynch, Morgan Guaranty, Shell, and Sears Roebuck. We also had a portfolio of illustrious British clients—Rolls-Royce, Schweppes, P&O, Guinness, Viyella, Austin cars, Rowntree, and the British Travel Association. Said *The Observer*, "Ogilvy has probably earned more dollars for Britain than any Briton since Winston Churchill won Lend-Lease."

I made some crashing mistakes. A friend asked me to handle the advertising for a fledgling company which made office machinery, but I had never heard of it and refused. My friend said I could buy shares in the company for a peppercorn. Again I refused. The name of the company was Xerox; they were soon spending $10,000,000 a year on advertising and the price of their shares has multiplied thirty-fold.

In addition to creating famous advertisements, I made speeches which attracted attention. I enraged a convention of automobile dealers in Las Vegas by telling them that the public regarded them as the most dishonest tradesmen in the country. I made a speech denouncing billboards as bad advertising and worse citizenship—"When I retire I am going to start a secret society of masked vigilantes who will travel about on silent motor bicycles, chopping down billboards at the dark of the moon." In another speech I attacked the governments of several countries for their incompetence in attracting tourists—"Wake up, Portugal! Get cracking, Switzerland! Pull your finger out, Italy! Move your ruddy arse, Germany!" And I rocked Madison Avenue by denouncing the time-honored system of compensation by commission as a conspiracy in restraint of trade.

Then I wrote a book which explained why Ogilvy & Mather was so successful. I did not expect it to sell more than four thousand copies, but I hoped it would attract new clients, and this it did. To my surprise, it also became a best-seller.*

I had arrived. *Fortune* published an article suggesting that I was a genius. CBS made a television program about me. I was invited to functions at the White House. I won the Parlin Award from the American Marketing Association. I was asked by the British Conservative Party to reorganize their publicity machine, which would have meant taking a sabbatical year from Madison Avenue and might well have opened the door to the political career which had once been my dream. But the invitation came too late; I had read enough memoirs of British politicians to lose interest in their machinations. I was made a Commander of the British Empire. I was offered the leading part in a Broadway play. Luther Hodges, the U.S. Secretary of Commerce, got me to help him

* *Confessions of an Advertising Man.* Since it was published, Ogilvy & Mather has grown sixteen-fold.

prepare the presentation he used in selling President Kennedy's Trade Expansion Act to Congress. Dorothy Schiff invited me to succeed her as publisher of the New York *Post*—an invitation she also extended to Adlai Stevenson and President Kennedy. Most bizarre of all, the Library of Congress asked me to give them my papers. (If I had not done so, this book would be longer. Being too far away and too lazy to consult my papers in Washington, I have to rely on my memory, which is patchy.)

But there was a fly in the ointment: if I were hit by a taxi, Ogilvy & Mather would vanish into thin air. Clearly it was time to stop behaving like a one-man band and to convert the agency into an institution.

I had been working under too much pressure. I wrote the prototype advertisements for most of our clients, and made the presentations to the prospective clients. I staggered from meeting to meeting—sales conventions which began on Sunday afternoons, breakfast conferences with the octogenarian Helena Rubinstein in her bedroom, lunches with Sam Bronfman of Seagram. Here is a page from my diary:

Got up at five o'clock, went to my study and did my homework—three brief-cases. At 7:30 took breakfast up to my wife.

Drove to the office. Commander Whitehead called. He wants to drop out of the Schweppes advertising. What the hell do we do for an encore? Houston called to discuss the next wave of Shell advertising.

Went to the screening room and inspected five new television commercials. Saw a couple of stockbrokers. They use the damnedest jargon on Wall Street. They start by "taking a position." Then they start "going in and out." Finally they have "repeated spasms of climactic selling."

Lunched in the office cafeteria and resisted the temptation to share a table with a pretty secretary. Talked to a humorless young man from the Harvard Business School.

At 2:00 I met with Bill Phillips who looks after General Foods, our biggest account. Bill has a problem. The first time Theodore Roosevelt tasted Maxwell House coffee, he exclaimed, "It's good to the last drop!" That's what we always say in our advertising. Now the lunatic lawyers demand that we *prove* Maxwell House is good to the last drop.

Rehearsed a new business presentation. Got home at 8:20. Dined and went back to my homework.

During weekends I wrote more than a hundred and fifty memoranda, letters, and notes. Every year I went to England and saw our British clients. The butler at the Rolls-Royce guest house entered my bedroom on a hot summer morning, without knocking. There lay my wife, sound asleep and naked as a jay. Poking his moon face into her ear, he shouted, "Poached or fried, madam?" Lord Mabane of British Travel sent his car to drive us to Rye, where he lived in Henry James's house; his chauffeur startled my wife by asking if she would like to suck one of his gums.*

On top of all this, I was doing free-lance work during vacations. The Omega watch people in Switzerland paid me $25,000 to spend four days telling them how to improve their advertising— and got their money's worth. *Reader's Digest* paid me $5,000 to write one advertisement for their magazine. So did *Holiday* and *The New Yorker*. O. M. Scott & Company paid me $130,000 for advice on how to market their lawn-care products. In some years I made more money moonlighting than I made at Ogilvy & Mather; I could never understand why my staff did not do the same thing.

In my spare time I was working as a volunteer for several good causes. John D. Rockefeller III

* English word for jujube.

and Clarence Francis recruited me as chairman of the Public Participation Committee of Lincoln Center, and for one year I presided over four meetings a week. When that was finished, Rockefeller asked me to be chairman of the United Negro College Fund; I went to work with high enthusiasm, but ran into a hornet's nest and resigned. I served as vice-chairman of a committee which advised British industry on how to increase exports to the United States. I joined the board of the New York Philharmonic, and in 1962 became a trustee of Colby College.

At the first meeting of the Colby Board I was given an honorary M.A.—my first and last college degree.* I took a passionate interest in Colby and developed eight bees in my bonnet:

---

* Not the last. Adelphi University has just made me a Doctor of Letters. The citation made me purr: "Yours has been the counsel of candor—insisting that good advertising does not make promises it cannot keep. You have set high standards of responsibility to the public. You are a great copy writer, bringing a richly furnished mind to the task, formed by a Spartan Scottish education. You have created unforgettable ideas in adult language. You have warned advertising writers against the assumption of public gullibility, and condemned 'flatulent puffery.' You have always known that creativity comes not by committee but from one good mind and seventeen drafts. Because you have brought good taste to salesmanship, because you have respected the consumer as a fellow human being, because you speak plainly in an age of twisted words, we are proud to name you, David Ogilvy, Doctor of Letters, honoris causa, with all the rights and privileges pertaining thereto."

133

1. A very large part of what students and teachers do in colleges and universities is sheer waste. When Dr. Gallup tested a cross-section of college graduates of all ages, he found that one third had not read a book of any kind during the previous twelve months.

2. The tutorial system at Oxford and Cambridge is far superior to the classroom system in American colleges.

3. Tenure should be abolished. It is imposed on universities by the American Association of University Professors, which is one of the most powerful trades unions in the country. The case for tenure revolves around the protection of teachers who advocate unorthodox theories. No doubt such protection is desirable, but it is even more desirable to protect students from incompetent teachers. A don can be terrific at the age of thirty-five, when he gets tenure, but an extinct volcano at the age of fifty. Pity the generations of students who are taught by extinct volcanoes. It is preposterous that tenure should be a *one-way* contract. If a professor cannot be sacked, he should also be unable to quit in search of richer pastures.

4. Colleges should reduce the number of courses to three. My heart bleeds for the students who are still obliged to take five. They have to work under such cruel pressure, and so superficially.

5. A professional psychiatrist should be on the staff at every college. A lot of parents still regard psychiatry as new-fangled nonsense—until their children drop out of college, or are sent to hospitals with a breakdown, or commit suicide. No student should be expelled (as I was) until he has had a few sessions with a psychiatrist. This would save a lot of them, and it is our duty to save them.

6. There is always a hue-and-cry to add new departments, but a college of limited resources cannot achieve the same degree of distinction in *all* its academic departments. I agree with the Oxford don who said that the strength of a college can be measured by the number of subjects it *refuses* to teach. New York University offers a course in "trapeze work, tumbling, juggling and miscellaneous acrobatics."

7. One of the most useful things we can teach students is to *write lucid reports*. If

135

you are going to be a businessman, you won't get far unless you can write properly—and very few college graduates can. If you are going to be a doctor, it will help if you can contribute lucid articles to medical journals.

8. I cannot understand the point of sending students home for four months every summer. If their fathers are farmers, they are needed to help with the harvest, but the vast majority would be better off with a vacation of four weeks than four months. Then we could graduate students in three years instead of four.

I had always supposed that college boards of trustees were the enemies of reform, but the Colby board was remarkably liberal and progressive. It was the faculty who obstructed progress.

The time had come for me to change gears and concentrate my energies on planning the long-term future of Ogilvy & Mather. So I gave up good works, stopped writing advertisements, cut myself off from contact with clients, refused all speaking invitations, and turned over the day-to-day management of the agency to younger partners. This made Ogilvy & Mather immeasurably stronger.

I began to perceive the really important opportunities, and now had the time to do something about them. First, I developed an international network, figuring that manufacturers who thought Ogilvy & Mather were the cat's whiskers in the United States might like to use our services in other parts of the world. The next step was to make Ogilvy & Mather a public company. This put me on easy street, but going public was not all beer and skittles. I had to watch helplessly while the market price of my remaining shares went up and down like a yo-yo. Our profits increased every year, but our shares fluctuated with the market.

When an advertising agency goes public, it commits itself to a policy of *perpetual growth.* You then have to resist the temptation to put profit ahead of service to clients. You also have to resist the temptation to diversify into other kinds of business. Those of our competitors who did not resist this temptation lost their shirts. We stuck to our knitting.

In the early days of Ogilvy & Mather, it did not take more than two or three inspiring officers to sustain an atmosphere of ferment and innovation, but with four thousand employees we needed a *hundred* leaders—to manage our offices and to preside over the creation of campaigns. The search for such leaders became my chief preoccupation. Once located, they were given a document which summarized my principles:

137

Never forget that the creation of remarkable advertising is the heart, liver, and lights of our business.

Advertising agencies are fertile ground for office politics. You should work hard to minimize them, because they absorb energy which can better be devoted to our clients. Here are some ways to control them:

1. Always be fair in your own dealings; unfairness at the top can demoralize an agency.
2. Never hire relatives or friends.
3. Sack incurable politicians.
4. Crusade against paper warfare. Encourage your people to air their disagreements *face-to-face*.

A vital factor in morale is *the posture of the boss*. If he is miserable, it will filter down through the ranks, and make the whole office miserable. You must always be contagiously cheerful.

Superior service to our clients depends on making the most of our people. Give them challenging opportunities, recognition for achievement, job enrichment, and the maximum responsibility. Treat them as grown-ups—and they will grow up. Help them when they are in difficulty. Be affectionate and human.

Never allow two people to do a job which *one* could do. George Washington observed, "Whenever one person is found adequate to the discharge of a duty by close application thereto, it is worse executed by two persons, and scarcely done at all if three or more are employed therein."

Encourage your staff to be candid with you. Ask their advice—and listen to it. Ogilvy & Mather offices should not be structured like an army, with overprivileged officers and underprivileged subordinates. Top bananas have no monopoly on ideas.

If you hire people who are bigger than you are, Ogilvy & Mather will become a company of giants; if you hire people who are *less* than you are, we shall become a company of dwarfs.

Encourage ferment and innovation. In advertising, the beginning of success is to be different, the beginning of failure is to be the same.

Try to make working at Ogilvy & Mather *fun*. When people aren't having any fun, they seldom produce good advertising. Kill grimness with laughter. Encourage exuberance. Get rid of sad dogs who spread gloom.

I subscribe to the Scottish proverb: HARD WORK NEVER KILLED A MAN. Men die of boredom, psychological conflict, and disease. They do not die of hard work. The harder people work, the happier they are. Agencies which frequently work nights and weekends are more stimulating.

Sustain unremitting pressure on the professional standards of your people. In our competitive business, it is suicide to settle for mediocre advertising.

The most priceless asset we have is the *respect of our clients*. This comes from the following:

1. Our offices are headed by men and women who command respect. Not phonies, zeros, or bastards.

2. We are honest in our dealings with clients. We tell them what we would do if we were in their shoes.

3. We treat our employees well, and they speak well of Ogilvy & Mather to their friends. Assuming that each employee has a hundred friends, 400,000 people know people who work here.

4. While we are responsible to our clients for sales results, we are also responsible to the public for the kind of advertising we bring into their homes. That is why we

must create advertising that is in *good taste*.

Our growth depends on our ability to develop a large cadre of able partners. Each of our offices has a *managing* partner. The total responsibility for the office rests on his shoulders. However, if he is wise, he will treat his lieutenants as equals. Only second-raters accept permanent subordination.

Our top management in each country should function like a roundtable, presided over by a chairman who is big enough to be effective in the role of *primus inter pares*, without having to rely on the discipline of a military hierarchy. This egalitarian structure encourages independence and responsibility. It reduces the agency's dependence on ONE MAN, who is often fallible, sometimes absent, and always mortal. And it insures continuity of style from generation to generation.

It is as difficult to sustain happy partnerships as to sustain happy marriages. Our partners should have these qualities:

1. Stability, guts under pressure, resilience in adversity, deep keels.
2. Brilliant brains—not safe plodders.
3. Commitment to hard work.

4. A streak of unorthodoxy.

5. The guts to face tough decisions, including firing nonperformers.

6. Inspiring enthusiasm.

7. Speed in grasping nettles.

It is important to spot people of unusual promise early in their careers, and to move them up the ladder *fast*. If you fail to promote young men of exceptional promise, they will leave us, and the loss of an exceptional man can be as damaging as the loss of a client.

It is desirable that the heads of all our offices should become personages in their communities. The best way for them to achieve this is by making remarkable speeches. If you make dull speeches, you will not be reported—and you will never be invited to address important audiences. If you make good speeches, you will be widely reported, and you will get your pick of audiences. Take a lot of trouble in preparing your speeches, and don't make more than two a year.

I discovered that almost everybody is frightened of his boss, *ex officio*, even if the boss is a milquetoast. When one man retired from Ogilvy & Mather, he told me that during his first three months in the agency he had been so frightened of me that he had to go to the bathroom every half hour. During my underling years, I lived in constant dread of being fired. I have always assumed that other people are subject to the same fear, so I never summoned anyone to my office without telling him what I wanted to talk about. If you ever find yourself faced with the ghastly job of sacking somebody, I offer you this advice:

1. Give him the bad news at the very beginning of the interview. It is cruel to lead up to it.
2. Don't tell your victim he is incompetent or repulsive. It is awful enough to be sacked; to have your self-esteem obliterated can ruin a man for life.
3. As soon as you have delivered the bad news, talk to the poor devil as if he were your brother. Tell him what you would do in his shoes.
4. End the interview by inviting him to lunch the following day. This makes him feel that dismissal does not imply personal rejection.

You will have to cope with the sibling rivalry of your henchmen. Dr. William Menninger thought that it was specially prevalent in advertising agencies. I heard him say:

A very special problem with the employees of an advertising agency is that you have to accumulate these creative, high-strung people and that you always find them extremely sensitive. Each one watches the other one very carefully to see if one gets a carpet before the other, to see if one has an assistant before the other, or to see if one makes an extra nickel before the other. It isn't that they want the carpet or the assistant or the nickel so much as it is the recognition of their standing with father.

When I was raising money for the Menninger Clinic, a management consultant who had been engaged to reorganize that Valhalla of psychiatry told me that the whole atmosphere was poisoned by the sibling rivalry between the two Menninger brothers.

The more power and patronage is concentrated at the top, the more virulent the sibling rivalry below. Louis XIV complained, *Toutes les fois que je donne une place vacante, je fais cents mécontents et un ingrat.*[*]

As the years passed, I was able to build a team of partners the like of which had never been seen in the advertising business—"gentlemen with brains." Some were more stable than others and some were uncomfortably self-serving, but all of

---

[*] Every time I give someone a job, I make a hundred people unhappy and one person ungrateful.

144

them were remarkable for their thrust and their independence. As befits the directors of a multinational company, they were a polyglot crew—five Americans, two Englishmen, one Canadian, one German, and one Australian. But, I am ashamed to say, none of them were women; it fell to my successor to redress that wrong.

As our billings burgeoned into the hundreds of millions, winning new accounts no longer sent me into ecstasies. By this time big ones were coming in without my participating in the presentations—notably Avon, the biggest of all cosmetic companies, and Hershey, the biggest of all chocolate companies.

We spent millions of dollars measuring the *results* of our campaigns. From this research we were able to isolate hundreds of positive and negative factors. No other agency had accumulated such a corpus of knowledge, and, as a result, they had no consistent discipline. They were forced to fly blind.

Ogilvy & Mather was my magnum opus, and I stuck to it for twenty-six years. When I finally abdicated, it was for three reasons:

1. In Jock Elliott we had a man whom my partners agreed would make an admirable

successor. He is a former copywriter, distinguished for his eloquence, judgment, and stability.

2. While my ivory tower had given me a perspective which bore fruit, my detachment from the daily rat race had made me a nonplaying captain, and this had disadvantages.

3. Because I cannot fly in airplanes, I could not visit our offices in Australia, New Zealand, Southeast Asia, India, Africa, or South America, and I was unknown to the men and women who worked in those offices. Bad.

I cannot end this account of my sojourn on Madison Avenue without saluting my clients. I liked almost all of them. The most inspiring was Ted Moscoso, the economic head of the Government of Puerto Rico and the mainspring of Operation Bootstrap. The first time I met Moscoso he asked, "What do we want Puerto Rico to become? An oasis of serenity with its roots in the Spanish tradition? An industrial beehive? A bridge between the United States and Latin America?" I suggested that the most urgent step was "to substitute a lovely image of Puerto Rico for the squalid image which now exists." This is what we did, and it helped Puerto Rico to escape from the poverty in which it had floundered for four hundred years.

When a manufacturer hires an advertising agency, it is sometimes an act of personal patronage; he believes that some individual within the agency would be a persuasive mouthpiece for his company. Such was the case when Max Burns and Monty Spaght awarded us the huge Shell account. Their patronage transformed Ogilvy & Mather from a boutique into a major agency; I did not let them down. Some of our clients became my friends—Commander Whitehead of Schweppes, Sir Colin Anderson of P&O–Orient, Arthur Houghton of Steuben Glass, Ellerton Jetté of Hathaway shirts, Edgar Cullman of General Cigar, Heinz Hoppé of Mercedes-Benz.

My greatest regret is that I was never able to persuade my partners to move our offices out of New York, London, Frankfurt into country towns like Princeton, Cambridge, and Salzburg. I argued that if the Mayo brothers could make the little town of Rochester, Minnesota, into a place of pilgrimage for sick people from all over the world, we could do the same thing. My partners thought I was nuts.

I learned eleven lessons on Madison Avenue:

1. You can divide advertising people into two groups—the amateurs and the professionals. The amateurs are in the majority. They aren't *students* of advertising. They guess. The pro-

fessionals don't guess, so they don't waste so much of their clients' money.

2. The difference between a great advertisement and an ordinary one can be as much as 19 to 1—when you measure them in terms of sales results.

3. It follows that the most important function in advertising is the *creative* function. But only one in ten of the people in agencies work in the creative department. The account executives outnumber the copywriters two to one. If you owned a dairy farm, would you employ twice as many milkers as cows?

4. Most of the products we advertise are bought by women, and used by women. But almost all the advertising is created by men and approved by men. Of seventy-three people installed in the Advertising Hall of Fame since it was established in 1949, only *one* has been a woman. This is crazy.

5. Too many people are involved in the advertising process. Too many levels of approval. Too many committees. Committees can criticize, but they cannot create. That is why so many advertisements and so many commercials look like the minutes of a committee meeting.

6. The worst way for a manufacturer to pick an agency is to invite speculative presentations. The only thing this measures is the agency's willingness to divert its best brains from the service of its *present* clients to the pursuit of *new* ones.

7. Unless your advertising contains a Big Idea, it will pass like a ship in the night.

8. You cannot *bore* people into buying your product, you can only *interest* them in buying it. You cannot save souls in an empty church.

9. The consumer is not a moron, she is your wife. Try not to insult her intelligence.

10. Advertising should be true, credible, and pleasant. People do not buy from bad-mannered liars.

11. The most important ingredient in any agency is *the ability of the top man to lead his troops.*

I had to sit through hundreds of meetings at which our clients argued about our advertising. I used to wonder how some of the big shots had gotten to the top of the tree. In some cases it was because their grandfathers had founded the corporation. In some cases it was political skulduggery which had won them the chairman's seat; I knew one who had bugged the offices of his rivals. Some were adept at solving problems. Some were said to be good decision-makers.

But I seldom came across a top man who showed any ability as a *leader*. All too many of them, far from inspiring their lieutenants, displayed a genius for emasculating them.

Conventional wisdom says that leadership is a function of three factors—the leader himself, the people he has to lead, and the situation. I saw successful heads of big corporations become heads of government departments, only to find that their brand of leadership did not work in Washington. I saw Generals flounder when they became heads of industrial corporations. I saw Americans who had been good leaders in New York fail to distinguish themselves when they moved to Europe; they could not adjust their style of leadership to fit the psychological needs of European subordinates.

Most of the top men in our client companies were much nicer than the men they had passed on their way up the ladder. But it depressed me to watch corporations reject executives who did not fit their conventions. When a brilliant friend of mine failed to make vice-president of Procter & Gamble, he was told that he was "too creative." Yet the best leaders have a strong element of "creativity"

150

in their characters. Instead of resisting innovation, which is the life blood of industrial companies, they personify it. Some of the best leaders are surprisingly odd characters when off duty; sexually chaotic and even alcoholic. On his honeymoon Lloyd George got another woman pregnant, and Winston Churchill drank as much as General Ulysses S. Grant.

On the evening before a major battle, Churchill's ancestor, the first Duke of Marlborough, was reconnoitering the terrain. He dropped his glove. Cadogan, who was his chief of staff, dismounted from his horse, picked up the glove and handed it up to Marlborough. After dinner that night Marlborough issued his final order: "Cadogan, put a battery of guns where I dropped my glove!"

"I have already done so," replied Cadogan. He had read Marlborough's mind, and *anticipated* his order. Cadogan was the kind of follower who makes leadership easy. I have known men whom nobody could lead.

I do not believe that *fear* is an ingredient in good leadership. People do their best work in a happy atmosphere. The physicists who first split the atom in Niels Bohr's laboratory were always playing practical jokes on each other.

Great leaders exude self-confidence. They are never petty. They are never buck-passers. They are resilient. They pick themselves up after defeat.

It does a company no good when its leader refuses to share his leadership functions with his lieutenants. The more centers of leadership you find in a company, the stronger it will become. That is how Ogilvy & Mather became strong.

[7]

The Light at the End of the Tunnel

U P to this point my life had been divided into a series of separate rooms: cooking in Paris, selling stoves in Scotland, polling for Hollywood, Secret Service, farming among the Amish, and building an advertising agency. I now had to find a room in which to end my days.

I set about it in a methodical way, rating six countries on twenty-four criteria. Which country offered the best climate for gardening? The most music? The best walking? The best bicycling? The best cooking?

My American friends could not understand why I finally chose France. The country which

153

had pleased Benjamin Franklin, Thomas Jefferson, Mary Cassatt, Edith Wharton, and Ernest Hemingway had fallen into disfavor. Surveys showed that Americans regard the French as immoral, and they dislike French cooking—"all those rich sauces." The bloody-minded ingratitude of De Gaulle, coupled with the malevolence of his policy toward Israel, had finally turned them off.

For some years my wife and I had been spending our vacations exploring France on bicycles. Bicycling is better than motoring. Your legs don't atrophy. You are not insulated from the landscape by steel and glass. Your contact with nature is absolute. You see more, and you smell more. You see the sky, and the French sky is worth seeing. You smell sweetbriar and wild strawberries and honeysuckle and foxes. You get gloriously thirsty pushing your bike up hills, and free-wheeling down the other side is a foretaste of heaven. At the end of the day you are saturated with fresh air and sleep like a baby.

In this way we had gotten to know France as few Frenchmen know it. The hills of Morvan, whose wet-nurses were esteemed above all others in the eighteenth century. In the Southwest, the road from Lacaune (with its rude fountain) to Belmont—the most beautiful road in France. The Dauphiné, where we could still get bread which tasted of bread. The roads above Thônes in Haute-

Savoie, where my father and I had tramped forty years before. And the marshes of La Vendée on the Atlantic. These are *obscure* places where you can ride all day without seeing more than a dozen cars, and cars are the enemies of bicyclists—honk, honk, honk. And never a foreign tourist. As an advertising man I had done my share in promoting tourism, but I sympathized with the Greek Orthodox Church when it caused the following prayer to be read from every pulpit:

> Lord Jesus Christ, Son of God, have mercy on the cities, the islands, and the villages of our Orthodox Fatherland, as well as the Holy monasteries, which are scourged by the worldly touristic wave. Grace us with a solution to this dramatic problem and protect our brethren who are sorely tried by the modernistic spirit of these contemporary western invaders.

There were other things I loved in France. The French genius for perpetual conversation. The absence of venereal disease—France has only thirty cases of gonorrhea per 100,000 population compared with more than two thousand in Atlanta and San Francisco. The swaggering military marches like "Sambre et Meuse," "Le Téméraire," and "Lorraine" made me quiver with vicarious patriotism.

155

If France could be so halcyon for three weeks every summer, why not all the year round? Thus ruminating, I heard that the Château de Touffou was for sale. The owner greeted me like a long-lost nephew and pressed me to stay the night. There were five wines at dinner. The next morning we were woken by a groom playing fanfares on the *trompe de chasse*. After breakfast we were shown the stables, with stalls for nineteen hunters. The château had thirty-seven bedrooms and seventeen bathrooms, three of which were in working order. A chapel, with a twelfth-century crucifix. A walled kitchen garden. A vineyard. Luncheon. Dinner. A second night. More fanfares.

Fifty years before, Sir Henry Royce had left the Rolls-Royce factory in England and gone to live in the South of France. There, free from interruption, he spent the last twenty years of his life, bombarding his factory with an endless stream of letters, directives, and drawings. Emboldened by this lofty precedent, I bought Touffou.

Some castles are by nature somber and forbidding. Touffou presents a smiling welcome to the world. It is partly its color—Ronsard called it apricot. It is also its lack of pretension, having been built before pretension was invented. The interior had been redecorated in 1898 in the gloomy Renaissance style which was then fashionable— dark red ceilings, brown walls, tapestries, and uncomfortable furniture. I painted the rooms white, put white carpets on the floor and bought comfortable sofas and chairs. In winter, logs blaze in the huge fireplaces. The rooms are always full of flowers; in summer they reek of lilies. The garden provides a procession of cherries, strawberries, raspberries, currants, gooseberries, figs, apples, pears, and persimmon.*

Touffou is curiously *fattening*. Some say it is the air, others blame the cook. Certainly the air is soporific, I think it contains laughing gas. The name Touffou is curious. When you hear it for the first time, it sounds like *tous fous*, which means *everyone is crazy*. It appears to have evolved from a series of mutations: Tolfol (old French for a plantation of beech trees) in the twelfth century, Thofo, Toffo, and Topho in the thirteenth century, Toutfou in the fourteenth century, and so on down to Touffou today.

The Keep, which is the oldest part of the house, was built three hundred and fifty years before Christopher Columbus was born. There are other castles of this vintage in France, but most of them had been battered into ruins by the end of the Middle Ages. Touffou has led a charmed life. During the Hitler war a fire broke out in one of

* But I cannot compete with my ancestor Sir Hector Mackenzie who gave the officers of a man-of-war thirty-four different varieties of pear when they dined at his house on the west coast of Scotland.

157

the towers, but it was extinguished by the German soldiers who were quartered in another part of the château. When the Royal Air Force tried to bomb Touffou in 1944, they hit the Château de Fou, ten miles away.

Thirty-six generations have lived in the room where I write these words. Its stone walls are ten feet thick. The Tour St. Jean, the Tour St. George, the Tour de l'Hotellerie and the Tour de la Chapelle were added in the fourteenth century. Under the chapel, there are diabolical prisons, and not far off a field where the owners of Touffou used to hang their enemies.

The first thing you notice when you come to Touffou (as I hope you will during July or August, when a pretty guide will show you round for four francs) is the view over the valley of the Vienne, which flows under our ramparts. However, it was the personality of the previous owner which made the most vivid impression on me when I first arrived. Enguerrand de Vergie was then seventy, a genial giant who devoted his life to the entertainment of his friends. He kept a hundred stag hounds and hunted twice a week throughout the winter; at the end of every hunt the Touffou butler produced a collation. When Enguerrand's friends were not hunting with him, they were shooting his pheasants, or visiting his racing stables, or being entertained by the theatrical troupes he brought from Paris on weekends. Some years before I met him, he had been galloping through a forest when a branch caught him across the chest and lifted him out of the saddle. His horse did not stop, his feet did not come out of his stirrups, and he was almost torn in half. Not long afterward the manager of the family business embezzled his fortune, and he had to sell everything he possessed. I could not bring myself to evict him from the house where he had lived all his life, so he lived with us, the life and soul of the establishment, until shortly before he died.

He had kept wild boar in the dry moat. The cook fed them by throwing garbage out of the kitchen window; on hot evenings in summer the stench was unforgettable. One amiable sow used to be carted to a nearby forest, released, and hunted by Enguerrand's hounds. After half an hour, she always got fed up, came back to the truck and was driven home. One day she had a litter of nine babies and escaped with them by opening a trapdoor which led from the moat to the courtyard.

The vineyard at Touffou produced six thousand bottles of wine a year. When I gave a glass of it to an expert from Bordeaux, he sniffed it, tasted it, gargled, and swallowed. "This isn't wine, it is *petrol*." So I tore up the vines and planted wheat. Enguerrand sold me the contents of the wine cellar, a distinguished collection from Bordeaux and Burgundy, but he had kept the whites too long and I had to throw away seven hundred bottles. "A man who dies with cork in his bottles is damned."

Enguerrand was convinced that the owner of Touffou at the time of the French Revolution had buried the family treasure before he was guillotined; he engaged water-diviners to locate it. The gardeners spent most of their time digging for it. Lacking faith in diviners, I sent to America for a metal detector, but the only treasure it detected was the tank for the heating oil. My next discovery was a tumulus which two local archaeologists identified as a tomb of the Iron Age. I dug it, but the only thing I found was a fragment of terra-cotta which was less than four hundred years old. The Iron Age tomb turned out to be an eighteenth-century rabbit trap.

Shortly after I acquired Touffou, its pastoral serenity was threatened by the Mayor of the village, a professor of mathematics at the University of Paris. He conceived the idea of turning our peaceful valley into a huge reservoir, complete with car parks, picnic grounds, and sports pavilions. An army of bulldozers would take four years to do the necessary excavations, and life at Touffou would be like a perpetual battle of tanks. Many of the people in the village owned land in the valley and welcomed the prospect of selling it at bonanza prices. The shopkeepers thought the project would attract tourists. Even the priest was in favor. When the Mayor became aware that I was the only person opposed to his dream, he came to see me. "Mr. Ogilvy, you have a long arm. I know for a fact that you summoned the Minister of Equipment to your office in New York and told him to veto my project." This was an exaggeration; I had seen the Minister, but on other business. The Mayor then threatened me. "The commune has a right of way through your property. If you continue to obstruct me, I will turn it into a three-lane highway." When this failed to move me, he tried corruption: "Your stepson is an architectural student. How would he like to design the pavilions?" I could only reply that I regarded myself as the custodian of Touffou, that it was the most important historical monument in Poitou, and that I felt compelled to protect it from vandalism. The fight continued for several years and was finally settled when the government classified the valley as a historical site. *Te Deum Laudamus.*

My custodianship of Touffou is no laughing matter. I discovered that the foundations rested on sand, with the result that the castle was slipping into the river; great fissures were appearing in the walls. It fell to me to extend the foundations downward until they rested on bedrock, a mining operation which took two years. Then the six-teenth-century frescoes on the ceiling of the Chambre François Premier began to disintegrate and I had to bring restorers from Florence to save them. Now the *roof* has given up the ghost; if any profit arises from the sale of this book, it will help to pay for a new one.

Is Touffou haunted? The other day I said to the gardener, "The tools have been kept in the Chaplain's house since time immemorial. I think it would be more convenient to keep them in the barn." He agreed and volunteered to help me move them. Just as we reached the door of the Chaplain's house, there was a terrific crash. *All the tools had chosen that moment to fall off the wall.*

The garden is on its way to becoming the most *fragrant* in France. I have divided it into a series of secret rooms enclosed by walls of evergreen hedge, and filled the rooms with plants which are notable for their smell—old-fashioned shrub roses, viburnums, daphne, philadelphus, lavender, magnolias, buddleia, Mrs. Sinkins pinks (in memory of my mother), pre-Spenser sweet peas, heliotrope, Trevithian daffodils, lilies, honeysuckle, lilac, nicotiana, acidanthera, choysia, and ancient orange trees in tubs.

The tourists show little interest in Touffou's history of architecture, but they love the prisons and the little museum of stag hunting. More than anything else they want to see the owner, but they never recognize the tatterdemalion pruning roses.

Our neighbors divide into three classes. The peasants, who now own motorcars and televisions and washing machines, are extraordinarily friendly; on my walks, they invite me into their houses and give me home-made liqueurs. The aristocracy devote their lives to shooting pheasants and hunting stags—forty hounds, thirty horses, thirty horsemen, and a hundred motorists versus one stag. They were brought up to think that gentlemen don't work. Some of them are brazenly unfaithful to their wives, but they never get divorced. Few of them went to a university, and they read nothing—not even the newspaper. But they have endearing manners and it is impossible to dislike them. They resemble the backwoods aristocracy in England a hundred years ago. Between the peasants and the aristocracy in this rigidly stratified society come the bourgeoisie—doctors, lawyers, professors at the University of Poitiers, industrialists, politicians, and merchants; civilized people.

Life at Touffou is close to paradise. The groom wakes you at dawn with a boisterous tune on the *trompe de chasse*. Ten minutes later the gardener brings you a brioche, a croissant, honey from our own heather, and a pot of coffee. You spend the morning gardening, or riding a horse in the forest, or bicycling, or floating in the pool, or bird-watching. How would you like to watch a Wall Creeper running up and down the apricot walls of Touffou, or hoopoes feeding on the lawn? You lunch in the garden in the shade of a seventeenth-century holly tree whose trunk has a circumference of fifty-seven inches. In the afternoon you row on the river, or play croquet, or swim. Then dinner, which is sometimes cooked by a retired chef from the Majestic in Paris.*

After dinner, you sit around and tell stories. The best of our storytellers, until he died two years ago, was Louis Spears, who had been a General in the British Army for fifty-seven years. As head of the Military Mission to Paris during the Kaiser's

---

* My star turn is *Carbonnade flamande*, a Belgian stew which was the *plat du jour* on Tuesdays at the Gaudin's Escargot Bienvenu in Soho during the thirties—my all-time favorite restaurant. Any tomfool can cook it to perfection: (1) Buy some very lean beef and get your butcher to slice it thin. Cut the slices into pieces the size of small dominoes. Brown them in hot fat. (2) Cut up as many onions as your eyes allow. Brown them in butter or margarine. (3) Make a brown roux. (4) Use the roux to thicken equal quantities of Campbell's beef consommé and beer. Escoffier, who was a culinary pedant, specifies old Lambic beer. (5) Season this unctuous sauce with salt, pepper, and a lot of *sugar*. Add some bay leaves. (6) Put the beef and the onions in an iron pot and cover with the sauce. Simmer until tender. This will take several hours—and smell superb. (7) Serve in a copper or earthenware casserole, with finely chopped parsley on top, for pretty. (8) The only vegetable which goes with *carbonnade flamande* is plain boiled potatoes.

164

war, he had accompanied the French cabinet on a visit to London. "The train stopped in Amiens. A message was handed in. One of the ministers read it. He said there had been a disaster. Eight hundred soldiers had been killed in a railway accident. Another minister said it was worse than a disaster, it was a *catastrophe*. Clemenceau asked, 'What is the difference between a disaster and a catastrophe? I will tell you: If President Wilson fell down a well, that would be a disaster, but if somebody pulled him out again, that would be a catastrophe.'"

During the battle of Verdun in 1916, it was decided that a battalion had to be sacrificed in an attempt to blunt the German attack. Clemenceau went to inspect them on the afternoon before the battle. Spears saw a group of *poilus*, who were aware that it was their last day on earth, go up to Clemenceau and give him a bunch of wildflowers. This was too much even for the Tiger; he took the flowers without a word, turned his back and cried. When he died, twelve years later, a dried bunch of flowers was found in his bedroom with a note directing that they should be placed in his coffin.*

In 1940 Churchill sent Spears to France as his personal representative. During the afternoon of June 16, Churchill telephoned to Reynaud in

* Clemenceau's *father*'s barber is still alive, aged one hundred and ten.

Bordeaux and proposed that France and Britain should no longer be two nations, but one Franco-British Union. The idea had originated with Jean Monnet, who hoped that it would give Reynaud and his colleagues the courage to fly to North Africa. But Pétain said it would be "fusion with a corpse," and surrendered to Hitler. Churchill himself had not been enthusiastic about the idea, and transmitted it only because the cabinet was in favor of it. Some years later he commented to Spears, "That was a lucky escape."

Spears left Bordeaux in the nick of time. There were three seats in his aircraft, one for the pilot, one for himself, and one empty one. He thought he had better give it to a Frenchman, and chose De Gaulle. When they arrived in England, Churchill was furious that he had not brought someone important.

One evening at Touffou Louis Spears told us this story: "In 1895 a Frenchwoman was arrested by the Jersey police and charged with having intercourse with a dog. She was tried, convicted, and sentenced to *death*, that being the penalty under Jersey laws. The French government protested to the Foreign Office, pointing out that in France the penalty for this crime would be a mere fine. Asquith, who was then Home Secretary, remonstrated with the Jersey authorities, but they were adamant. The only way to stop the sentence being carried out was to persuade Queen Victoria to issue a reprieve, but Lord Rosebery, the Prime Minister, could not bring himself to explain the case to the Queen, so it was decided to include the reprieve in a sheaf of army promotions. The old Queen duly signed it without inquiring as to the facts, but the reprieve had to be registered by the Jersey parliament and that august body was on vacation. By this time the Cabinet in London was entirely preoccupied with the case. At their meeting on the morning before the hanging was to take place, the First Lord of the Admiralty spoke up: 'Prime Minister, perhaps you had better allow me to deal with this.' So agreed. Late that night a gunboat party was put ashore on Jersey. They stormed the castle of Mont-St.-Orgueil, released the prisoner, took her on board and steamed at full speed to the French coast, where they pushed her overboard. She swam to liberty."

And so the days pass at Touffou, interrupted only by the chattering of the telex. While no longer chairman of Ogilvy & Mather, I am still on the board, with the same rights that Walter Bagehot thought a constitutional monarch should have: "The right to be consulted, the right to encourage and the right to warn." I see all the campaigns created by our fifty-five offices, praising the good ones and damning the bad. Once a month I stir my stumps and go on a round of visits to Ogilvy & Mather offices and the Swiss headquarters of the World Wildlife Fund. Last year I got as far as Persia and had two audiences with the Shah; he listened with extraordinary concentration to my proposals, but I was shot down by his staff. I am no longer the salesman that I used to be. But I can smell the flowers.

[8]

A Forest Full of Surprises

J U L I U S   R O S E N W A L D , who made a huge fortune as head of Sears Roebuck, once said, "I never could understand the popular belief that because a man makes a lot of money he has a lot of brains. Some very rich men who made their own fortunes have been among the stupidest men I have ever met in my life. Rich men are not smart because they are rich. They didn't get rich because they are smart. Don't ever confuse wealth with brains."

Gentle reader, do you know what your IQ is? I had always supposed mine to be about 145, below the genius level but normal for professional and administrative types. But I recently tested myself and scored 96, which is normal for *ditch diggers*.

Nor has this been my only handicap. At the age of nine I contracted asthma, and this crippling disease did not leave me until I was middle-aged. I have more than my share of phobias. I am frightened of the sea. My earliest memory is being rowed out a hundred yards from the beach and yelling to the boatman, "Take me in, damn you, I'm out of my depth." Twenty-five years later, in a slight swell outside Newport, Jerry Lambert was woken at four o'clock one morning by my shouts on the deck of his 185-foot schooner, "Man the boats! Every man for himself!" I am so terrified of elevators that when I worked in Bill Stephenson's office on the thirty-sixth floor of Rockefeller Center, I never went out to lunch. But my most acute phobia is for turbulence in aircraft, a curse which no amount of grog, hypnosis, or psychiatric pills can exorcise. On those rare occasions when I am forced to travel by airplane, I never forget for a minute that the trains below are four times as safe.

The only games I can play are croquet and Attaque; no golf or tennis or bridge or chess. The only dances I can dance are the polka and the galop. I read at a snail's pace, but do not move my lips. I have no small talk, but am the best listener you can ever hope to meet. My silliest vice is that I go to cumbersome lengths to avoid everything that is unpleasant, like uncongenial society. As a young man I was conspicuously handsome, although I was not aware of it at the time. In any case, it was no particular advantage; as the Spanish proverb has it, *el hombre como el oso, mientras más feo más hermoso*—as with bears, so with men, the uglier the handsomer. When John Wilkes, the ugliest man in eighteenth-century England, was asked to explain his notorious success with women, he replied, "It takes me half an hour to talk my face away."

My idea of heaven is the same as Keats's— "Give me books, fruit, French wine, and fine weather."

I am much given to hero-worship, and these have been my heroes:

Francis Mackenzie Ogilvy, my grandfather.

Francis Fairfield Ogilvy, my brother, was seven years older than me. At many turning points in my life I was the beneficiary of his patronage: he got me my first job in advertising, introduced me to the Secret Service, and raised the capital which made it possible for me to start Ogilvy & Mather. But we were very different kinds of men. He did not share my taste for the limelight, or my horror of alcohol. He was wildly extravagant where I am a miser. When he died I wrote, "A quirk in the character of all Ogilvys makes it difficult for us to say anything pleasant about each other; we play an elaborate game of sarcastic denigration, to conceal our mutual devotion. But, in death, I allow myself to admit that Francis was the great hero of my life, and, for the last thirty years, my best friend."

Sir Humphry Rolleston, who was expelled from school as a dunce, lived to become Regius Professor of Medicine at Cambridge, president of the Royal College of Physicians, and Physician Extraordinary to the King. Uncle Humphry—he married my father's sister Leila—was unique among doctors in that he never kept a patient waiting. A man of immense erudition, he quoted from three hundred authors in his Harveian oration on cardiovascular diseases. When he died the *British Medical Journal* wrote, "All the best traditions of the profession, its courtesy, its learning, its uprightness and devotion to truth were in him."

Monsieur Pitard, head chef at the Majestic. A great professional and the most terrifying man I have known; but an inspiring leader of a hot-tempered brigade.

172

Harry Roberts, a Cornishman who practiced medicine in the London slums on Mondays, Tuesdays, and Wednesdays, and spent the rest of every week in the country—gardening, writing, and talking to his friends.

Sir William Stephenson, who was one of the most effective members of the intelligence community in the Hitler war. Quiet, ruthless, and loyal.

Milton Slaymaker, a carpenter who presided over every Amish barn-raising in Lancaster County for fifty years and never had a fatal accident.

Ira Stoltzfus, the Amish bishop whose awesome authority over his eleven children and his church was matched only by his humor and his wisdom. If he had not been born Amish, he would have become Chief Justice.

George Gallup, who taught me how to use research in advertising. A shy genius, with infectious curiosity.

Arthur Houghton, who made Steuben Glass what it is today, and employed me to do his advertising. Philanthropist, curator of rare books at the Library of Congress, supreme breeder of Angus bulls, chairman of the New

York Philharmonic and president of the Metropolitan Museum. He has made the most of being rich.

Teodoro Moscoso, who was the architect of Puerto Rico's Operation Bootstrap. Nothing I ever suggested to him was wasted.

Raymond Rubicam, the best of all advertising men. In the early days of Ogilvy & Mather he was my mentor, excoriating me with brutal candor when I created bad campaigns and praising me to the skies when I did good ones.

John Loudon, who, as head of Royal Dutch Shell, was my client, and became my friend. Of all the tycoons I have known, this Dutch aristocrat has the most gentle manners and the wisest head.

Marvin Bower, who made McKinsey what it is today—the most effective and influential firm of management consultants in the world. From him I learned lessons which improved my management of Ogilvy & Mather.

My business partners never found me an easy bedfellow. A psychologist who had interviewed them told me that "working with you seems to be like walking in a forest full of surprises." Graphologists, in whom I have great faith, say that my handwriting reveals me to be unpredictable, impulsive, impetuous, intolerant, anxious, energetic, audacious, assertive, sensitive, benevolent, enthusiastic, tough—and tormented. I am all of these.

It is the fashion for writers of autobiography to reveal the secrets of their private lives. Bertrand Russell, for example, goes into detail about his affair with Ottoline Morrell, even telling you that she broke it off because she could not stand his bad breath. I have spared you such revelations.

Friends? Many of my dearest friends have been gathered to their ancestors. Patrick Bakker, a Dutch painter who was my bosom companion in Paris forty-seven years ago, died young. Sir Paul Butler, Caroline Ruutz-Rees, Bill Smith of Ipswich, Ronnie Tree, Larry Kubie, and Walter Maynard are in their graves. Each time I have moved from one "room" to another, I have lost touch with the dramatis personae of the previous room. Nancy de Selincourt, Oliver Hill and the Mathias family in England; Gracie Lambert, the Gallups and the Goulds in Princeton; Jane and Jack Howrey in Washington; my Amish friends in Pennsylvania; and, finally, the friends of my years in New York: Augusta Maynard, Pauline and Francis Plimpton, Edmund and Marion Goodman, Alfred and Mary Winslow Jones, Jean and Howard Clark, Jane and Cass Canfield. Only

175

three friendships have survived the changing geography of my life for more than forty years: Wendy Beck, Margot Wilkie, and Sir Paul Reilly of the Design Council. However, my richest vein of friendship has been among my partners in Ogilvy & Mather. While I am no longer in daily touch with them, my role as the company's Holy Spook brings us together four or five times a year, and absence makes my heart grow fonder.

Horace wrote my epitaph, and Dryden translated it into English:

Happy the man, and happy he alone,
He, who can call to-day his own:
He who, secure within, can say,
To-morrow do thy worst, for I have lived to-day.

Index

Index

Index

David Ogilvy

David Ogilvy was born in 1911 in West Horsley, England. Educated at Fettes College, Edinburgh, and Christ Church, Oxford, he started his career as an apprentice chef in the kitchens of the Hotel Majestic in Paris. He went on from Paris to sell stoves in Scotland, and later emigrated to America to become Associate Director of Dr. George Gallup's Audience Research Institute at Princeton.

During the Second World War, Mr. Ogilvy was on Sir William Stephenson's staff in British Security Coordination. After the war, he founded the advertising agency known today as Ogilvy and Mather. Mr. Ogilvy and his wife live in France. He is the author of the very successful *Confessions of an Advertising Man.*